CURRENT CONTROVERSIES IN MARKETING RESEARCH

CURRENT CONTROVERSIES IN MARKETING RESEARCH

Edited by
Leo Bogart

For
The Market Research Council

WARNER MEMORIAL LIBRARY
EASTERN COLLEGE
ST. DAVIDS, PA. 19087

MARKHAM PUBLISHING COMPANY / CHICAGO

9-25-91

HF 5415.2 .B58

Current controversies in
marketing research

MARKHAM SERIES IN MARKETING

Bogart (editor), *Current Controversies in Marketing Research*
Alexis,Holloway,and Hancock (editors), *Empirical Foundations of Marketing: Research Findings in the Behavioral and Management Sciences*

COPYRIGHT © 1969 BY MARKHAM PUBLISHING COMPANY
ALL RIGHTS RESERVED
PRINTED IN U.S.A.
LIBRARY OF CONGRESS CATALOGUE CARD NUMBER 68:19357

Introduction

The mark of maturity in a profession may well be found at the point where the gap between theory and practice is recognized and confronted. This point may now have been reached in the field of marketing research, in which most of the published literature deals either with an exposition of methods on "how to do it" or an attempt to systematically digest the findings which turn up.

The papers gathered in this volume represent a somewhat different approach. They focus on some of the outstanding issues on which many sound practitioners of marketing research are in disagreement. Some of these controversies reflect the growing pains of a field in the process of evolution; some perhaps reflect the inherent difficulties of any craft which involves the manipulation and interpretation of human behavior.

Most of the papers in this book (those by Berelson, Baxter, Sheatsley, Frankel, Zeisel, Barton, and Ehrenberg) were originally delivered before the monthly meetings of the Market Research Council during the 1965–1966 season, at which time I was president.

The Council, a limited membership organization of senior executives in marketing and marketing research, has met once monthly for over 40 years to hear distinguished speakers discuss various aspects of the profession. These papers have been gathered and edited under the sponsorship of the Council as part of its program to support the advancement of science in marketing. (A previous volume, *Models, Measurements and Marketing,* edited by Peter Langhoff, was similarly published for the Council by Prentice-Hall in 1965.)

Along with their counterparts in the traditional fields of product research and development, marketing researchers represent a unique phenomenon in business life: they are a corps of scientifically trained and professionally oriented people within a corporate structure which is essentially devoted to profit objectives quite different from those of science and the professions. In its early days, marketing research represented a glorified form of business record-keeping in the shape of distribution and sales analysis. It was inconceivable for the researcher's professional goals to be inconsistent with managerial profit goals. However, the extraordinary burgeoning of marketing research during the postwar period has been accompanied by a subtle change in the character of its practitioners.

Directly, this change has reflected the infusion of small numbers of strategically placed psychologists and sociologists into the field as specialists in consumer attitudes and survey methodology. Perhaps even more significantly, the social sciences have played an increasing part in conventional business-school marketing curricula and in the after-hours reading of otherwise untrained marketing research practitioners. As I suggest at greater length in the first paper of this book, the market researcher's role in business involves an essential dilemma to the degree that he defines himself as a social scientist. The professional goals of a scientist include the ideal of social service and the independent search for truth, and these goals may not be altogether consistent with the researcher's assignment or motivations as a businessman.

The growth of market research has also brought new problems which arise not from the scientific overtones of the profession, but from its trade aspect. An increasing number of interviews are being conducted, thus creating greater demands on the public which market researchers use as their basic source of information. New problems arise in the public relations of the profession, in the relations of researchers to their own field staffs, and in the relations between research organizations and clients. The conflicts that arise from these problems inevitably lead to questions and demands for standards by which proper and improper procedures may be distinguished.

Curiously enough, resistance to the adoption of codes of standards has not come mainly from the researchers of marginal ability or questionable ethics. Some of the stiffest opposition has come from the ranks of practitioners of the highest skill and integrity, who believe that any code represents an arbitrary imposition of values which contradicts the scientific spirit of constant challenge and inquiry.

The three codes reproduced in the appendix to this volume represent different approaches to solutions of the same basic problems. All express similar principles with different degrees of specificity. The American Association for Public Opinion Research was first to adopt a code and has enforced it effectively in several cases, in spite of the fact that the offenders were not members of the Association itself.

The codes of the American Association for Public Opinion Research and of the World Association for Public Opinion Research offer an interesting contrast. The W.A.P.O.R. code had to be phrased in a way that covered the special problems of survey research in comparatively underdeveloped areas of the world, as well as in areas where research was established and accepted. The primary purpose of the W.A.P.O.R. code is not so much to discourage malpractice in research as to provide benighted governmental authorities with "official" evidence that the researcher belongs to a legitimate and respected profession and as such has the right to interview without hindrance from the police. In short, the emphasis in the W.A.P.O.R. code was not on keeping researchers in line, but on establishing their professional right to ask questions as part of a generally understood international charter of free speech.

Although the Market Research Council has no code, it has adopted a series of position statements on ethical issues. These are also included in the appendix.

There is one significant but controversial issue in marketing research which is not considered at all in this volume. Within the past few years, the computer has revolutionized marketing research by providing a vast, almost inexhaustible, capacity to manipulate data. The computer's capacity to produce complex statistical tables from a given set of data is out of all proportion to the research profession's capacity to generate data out of original field work.

The most costly part of computer usage involves not the actual time that the machine spends spinning its wheels, but the time devoted by human beings to the preparatory programming. Because of this, there is a natural tendency to take whatever limited data are available for processing and subject them to all the analytical squeezing of which the computer is capable. The computer has spawned a new generation of syndicated services which collect and correlate marketing and media data. The results, printed out in the computer's neat and mechanically laid-out tables, suggest a precision which is not necessarily warranted by the quality of the original input, which consists of the answers that people originally give to an interviewer's questions.

Most corporate expenditures in marketing research today are devoted to the measurement of brand share or audience share on a continuing and repetitive basis. Minute differences in these figures, from one reporting period to the next, become the subject of great speculation and anxiety. This represents another reason why researchers frequently turn to the computer to manipulate trivial data, instead of turning their attention to bigger problems with less elaborate and sophisticated aids.

The computer has brought popularity to scaling, factor analysis, and other highly involved techniques which require extensive and formerly time-consuming mathematical exercises. As a result, mathematicians have moved into the forefront of marketing researchers. Mathematicians are trained in the art of logical statement; they are skilled at extrapolating data, constructing models, and preparing optimum estimates from limited evidence. But such skills, valuable as they are in handling data already at hand, are of slender utility in providing insight into the processes of human behavior and motivation which are at the root of most marketing research.

The chief controversy in marketing research today may, therefore, be the unarticulated one between those who regard survey evidence essentially as an extension of the "hard data" of production and sales statistics, and those who look upon the same evidence as an uncertain and shifting reflection of the human spirit and consider consumer research itself as only one small aspect of the study of man.

New York
November 15, 1967

Leo Bogart

Contents

PART ONE

Researcher and Client

Marketing research is a profession which shares with the other social sciences the scientific tradition of inquiry for knowledge's own sake. At the same time, market research is a thriving component of contemporary business, earning its keep through the hard-headed competitive demands of the market itself. The researcher, argues this paper, is a man in the middle, facing the dilemma posed by these two conflicting roles. That dilemma is echoed in many of the papers in this volume.

The author is Executive Vice-President and General Manager of the Bureau of Advertising of the American Newspaper Publishers Association and is a former president of both the American and World Associations for Public Opinion Research, as well as of the Market Research Council.

1. The Researcher's Dilemma*

LEO BOGART

The marketing researcher faces two ways: toward his professional ethos, and toward business achievement. As with everyone else in this world, his life is a constant progression of decisions about means and ends. (See Figure 1.)

1. As a professional, he gets pleasure out of doing his job well; and his preoccupation with techniques or means leads him toward the goals of craftsmanship.
2. But the professional researcher may also have been trained to think of himself as a scientist concerned with the pursuit of truth for its own sake as an ultimate value.

FIGURE 1
Means and Ends

	Means	*Ends*
Professional Orientation	1. Craftsmanship goals	2. Scientific goals
Business Orientation	3. Bureaucratic goals	4. Corporate goals

3. As a businessman, his short-run concern with means (and the pun is intended) usually leads him to build his own empire. Like most white-collar men in a profit-oriented society, he wants to advance his own career; he wants to enhance his own research firm or his own research department with respect to the total bureaucratic structure of management, clients, or rival departments in his own business. He protects himself and his associates by struggling to raise the importance of the research function.
4. In a broader perspective as a businessman, he is also concerned with ends and with the corporate goals of sales and gain, to which facts about the market may make a contribution.

*Reprinted from *Journal of Marketing*, Vol. 26, No. 1 (January, 1962), pp. 6–11.

All four of these different sets of goals may be congruent, but more often they are not. This is at one and the same time a source of stimulation, of anxiety, and of self-analysis.

We often hear the problems of researcher and management defined as a conflict of interests between specialist and generalist—but this is an oversimplification. Isn't a man with the broad business experience and competence of an Elmo Roper, a George Gallup, or an Alfred Politz at least as much of a generalist as the corporation president who has dealt all his life with the problems of a single industry?

The researcher in a large organization typically moves ahead by developing his other skills—as a general administrator, or as an expert on the broad problems of the industry in which he is working. Typically his progress is measured by the extent to which he can leave his purely research functions behind him. In this respect, the problems he himself faces and presents to his management are equivalent to those faced by other kinds of specialists in a large enterprise.

Peter Drucker has stated the problem brilliantly:[2]

> As long as there have been organized armies the great majority of officers who have become majors have retired as majors. It has always been true that not everybody can become a general. But there is a difference between a major who remains a battalion commander while another battalion commander moves on to become general, and a meteorologist-major who remains a major because this is the furthest any meteorologist can go under the existing system. The first may feel personally aggrieved, may feel that he is a better man than the general, and that he owes his bad luck to favoritism and intrigues, if not to the proverbial stupidity of the higher-ups. But his job, whatever his personal feelings, is a subordinate job; it is within a much smaller sphere, the same kind of job as the general's. The meteorologist's job, however, is not subordinate. It is a specialist's job requiring highly advanced scientific knowledge. In his own field he is asked to function as a general while enjoying the status only of a major. . . .
>
> Mercenaries can be satisfied with pay, promotion or plunder. Professional people if they want to respect themselves must see their work as serving no mean end, and as part of a grand design.

It is a lack of certainty about the shape of the grand design, and about his own place in it, which often gives the researcher in business a tentative and ambiguous personality in his dealings with management.

---

[1] Jack O. Vance, "Why Not Promote the Marketing Research Manager?," *Journal of Marketing*, Vol. 23 (January, 1959), pp. 253–256. A dissenting view is that of Stanley L. Payne, "Should the Marketing Research Manager Be Promoted?," *Journal of Marketing*, Vol. 24 (July, 1959), pp. 59–61.

[2] Peter F. Drucker, *Landmarks of Tomorrow* (New York: Harper & Brothers, 1959), pp. 85–87.

SPECIALIZATION AND DIVIDED LOYALTY

Of all the thousands of people engaged in marketing research today, there are probably very few whose livelihood derives solely from their technical skills in designing and executing research projects. Their major contribution generally comes from the knowledge they acquire in the course of their work about particular businesses or marketing institutions. Or it comes from their acquaintance, through training or experience, with the principles of human behavior and motivation in terms of which data can be systematically collected and analyzed.

Many marketing researchers suffer from divided loyalties. They are also (depending on their original graduate training) statisticians or mathematicians, economists, sociologists, geographers, psychologists; or depending on their business apprenticeship, they are advertising men, cosmetics men, automobile men, appliance men, beer men, newspaper men.

As research is applied to a wider range of marketing problems, it loses its formerly generic character and becomes highly sub-specialized. Twenty years ago, even ten years ago, there was no type of marketing study that a capable researcher could not do, or at least would not consider himself capable of doing.

By contrast, a well-rounded research department in a large advertising agency today has to be able to handle a broad range of assignments: economic forecasts and sales analyses . . . evaluation of merchandising methods and distribution systems . . . motivation studies which involve the use of personality-testing techniques borrowed from clinical psychology . . . as well as the more traditional types of consumer surveys and copy tests. The research people must have the "know-how" to set up a probability sample . . . to weight tabulations . . . to perform complicated scaling analyses . . . to run psychological experiments . . . to set up a mathematical programming scheme for operations research on distribution methods.

Then, of course, the research department is also expected to be a storehouse of information on particular product fields, and on such advertising subjects as media selection, creative production, merchandising, sales promotion, and market planning. In research, as in any other type of business management, there is an important place for the generalist who knows the areas of his own ignorance, and can use the skills of the specialists and put their findings to work.

The increased tendency to rely on specialists carries with it the problem that the research man and the user of research are no longer speaking the same language. But in bridging the communications gap, a new danger arises, which is that inherently complex knowledge may be reduced to a simplicity of statement which distorts the essence of research conclusions.

PROBLEMS OF PROFESSIONAL STATUS

How legitimate is the aspiration of researchers to professional status? Webster's New Collegiate Dictionary defines the word "profession" as follows:

> PROFESSION—The occupation, if not commercial, mechanical, agricultural, or the like, to which one devotes oneself; a calling . . . The body of persons engaged in a calling; as "the *profession* distrust him." *(Sic!)*

Notice the qualification—"the occupation, *if not commercial!*"

Recently interviewers for a leading marketing research firm were enjoined from their doorbell ringing by the police of a California community, under the provisions of an ordinance which forbids soliciting for commercial purposes. When the firm protested that its interviewers were merely gathering information, and not selling anything, they were asked, "You sell the information, don't you?" There is no ready answer to that question.

The phrase "marketing research" is used to cover an enormous range of disciplines and skills, as well as sheer clerical labor. Where does one draw the fine line in professionalism between the project director and the interviewer, and between the economic forecaster and the compiler of sales statistics?

How does one define the professional community between the econometrician and the clinical psychologist, both of whom solve marketing problems and may refer to themselves as marketing researchers?

A great deal of what passes for marketing research might far better be characterized as marketing intelligence, since it involves no analytical comparisons and has no reference points in systematic theory. It gathers data for their own sake, rather than testing hypotheses and thus coming to generalizations.

Many of the technical skills required in research, such as those involved in sampling, interviewing, tabulating, and the like, are administrative rather than professional skills. Research, when it is repetitive and routinized, is transformed into the assembly of intelligence. This can be true of sales analysis, the ratings of television and radio programs, store auditing, the measurement of competitive advertising, and similar activities. These kinds of work are carried on primarily to answer the question, "How are we doing?" or "What's happening?" rather than to penetrate the mysteries of consumer or audience behavior. In this respect, their value is akin to that of clipping interesting items from the trade press, getting copies of the annual reports of competitors, or having lunch occasionally with old acquaintances who have gone over to a rival firm.

If the marketing researcher considers himself a professional, is not every intelligent and enlightened businessman entitled to make the same claim if he has attended a summer management-training institute or is a faithful reader of the *Harvard Business Review* and the *Journal of Marketing?*

Those who do not share the title or training of the marketing researcher may consider themselves, and with reason, to be quite as well qualified as he is to offer explanations of shifting consumer tastes, or to graph sales trends in different territories, and to draw the correct conclusions.

PROFESSIONAL STATUS AND PROFESSIONAL STANDARDS

Who is a proper professional, and who is not?[3]

In the case of older professions like medicine or law, there are accepted procedures of certification, which require minimum levels of training through education or apprenticeship of a specified kind. In addition, there is a pledge of adherence to a code of behavior, the violation of which may set in motion an orderly process of investigation and sanction.

Where the attempt has been made, as in the American Association for Public Opinion Research, to introduce similar standards into the field of marketing research, resistance has centered on the admitted lack on the part of the organization of any serious requirements for membership other than "interest" in the subject.

A code, says the opposition, implies some clear-cut agreement on what the standards of procedure are, and is inappropriate for a field which is fraught with technical controversies and characterized by short-lived technical fads and fashions. And if there are no agreed-upon standards of procedure (runs the argument), does not a code become merely an injunction against business immorality, already forbidden by law?

In attitude research, the difference between unethical behavior and mere incompetence is often strictly a matter of motivation, and who is a proper judge of that? What may be a gross infraction of professional ethics on the part of a skilled practitioner may be merely an expression of naïveté or ineptitude on the part of a less talented one.

Even among the partisans of formalized standards, there is no agreement as to what form they should take. Do we want a "thieves' code" of our own to set the boundaries on our conduct, a hortatory code that merely glowers down at us from its frame on the wall? Or do we want a code with teeth in it, with specified punishments for specified offenses?

FOUR TYPES OF ETHICAL PROBLEMS

We may distinguish four types of ethical problems in marketing research, any or all of which a code must cover.

One relates to the *researcher's honesty* in doing what he purports to do.

This is no different from any other aspect of business ethics, or of personal morality for that matter. One may occasionally run across the case of a "researcher" who produces a "report" on fabricated findings, just as there are occasional cases of interviewers who cheat by filling out the questionnaires themselves. In pre-Castro Cuba there was at least one firm which, for a fee, would provide a handsomely engraved certificate attesting that the "Court of Public Opinion" held the client or his products in whatever kind of high esteem might be desired (with no extra charge for percentages).

[3] Steuart Henderson Britt, "Advertising—Is It Business or Profession?," *Printers' Ink,* Vol. 255 (May 18, 1956), pp. 27–29.

The second kind of ethical problem relates not to outright falsification of findings, but to *distortion or selection of research techniques* in order to produce whatever findings are desired.

The dishonesty lies in the way in which the research is done to prove a point, whether this be the superior effectiveness of a particular advertising medium, or the preference of nine out of ten leading throat specialists for a particular brand.

If a survey finds that 5 per cent of the public read a particular magazine and if a research report says that 95 per cent read it, this represents an ethical violation under the first of our headings. But suppose that instead of falsifying the figures, we start out with a false or dubious premise and then gather statistically accurate data to support it. Or suppose that both our initial premises and our data are sound, but that we use only part of them in our report, and conveniently forget whatever findings contradict the ends we have in mind.

It is extremely difficult to draw the line between false promotional research and the perfectly useful kind which merely demonstrates a valid point that redounds to someone's credit: Magazine Z *does* reach a larger number of potential customers than do its competitors; the agency's recommendations *were* well-founded; throat specialists ordinarily *do* prefer to smoke Brand A (and not merely because they were mailed a free carton the week before the survey).

The line between proper and improper practice arises at the point where any disinterested researcher, starting with the same objective questions of fact, and selecting his techniques of investigation with an open mind, might be expected to come up with the same answers.

Thus, the researcher faces another type of ethical problem, which is a matter of *business judgment.*

At what point should he refuse to undertake projects which he is certain, in advance, will fail to yield the information his client or employer is after? This kind of problem arises whenever a client chooses to define a problem in terms that the researcher cannot accept.

An example would be the situation in which the researcher thinks a problem calls for a study of distribution and inventories, but he is instructed instead to study advertising appeals. Often this type of situation arises out of the client's desire to save money on research, by reducing a complex marketing problem to a single simple problem.

In this kind of a situation, the researcher's role as a professional and his role as a practical businessman may lead him into sharp conflict. When his client says (in the researcher's judgment, naively), "Here's what I want to know and here's how I want you to do it," should the researcher (if he deems the means inappropriate to the end) refuse to take the job, knowing that someone else will take it? Or should he consider his conscience clear after he has given his full measure of sound advice and delivered the necessary protestations? Does bad research drive out the good when there is probably someone who will do what is required for less money, and without any aggravating expressions of hesitation about the value of the project?

The fourth ethical problem concerns the *relationship of the researcher to the people he interviews.*

For research to be valid, it is often necessary to veil the true purpose and sponsorship of a survey from the respondents (often, indeed, from the interviewers as well). The reason for this is simply that the answers people give to questions may be influenced if they know why and for whom the questions are being asked. Yet some distinguished social scientists have expressed their opposition to the practice of disguising the real reasons for a question on the grounds that it involves an unprofessional breach of faith.

In experimental psychology, there is a long-standing tradition of giving human experimental subjects a fictitious rationale which differs from the true purpose of the experimenter; but it is also part of the tradition to enlighten the subjects regarding the true purpose once the experiment is concluded. In marketing surveys, this type of revelation rarely takes place, but the demands on the respondents are usually far less than those on the people who act as subjects in a psychological experiment. (In its most innocuous form, "deceit" in the marketing research questionnaire may be found in the dummy questions on irrelevant matters which are often asked to deflect the respondent's attention from the real purpose of the interview. This might be contrasted with those psychological "tests" in which the subject's presumed collaborator actually has the mission of sabotaging his efforts.)

On this point, too, it is difficult to know where to draw the line between deception and discreet silence. The manifest content of an interview schedule may bear only passing resemblance to the true intentions of the researcher, which he pursues by interpretation and analysis. Must we really explain, when we ask the respondent to agree or disagree with the statement, "Prison is too good for sex criminals; they should be publicly whipped or worse,"[4] that it is really the authoritarianism of his personality we are investigating, and not public opinion on crime and punishment?

PRESSURES ON THE RESEARCHER

Every researcher who has carried out a pilot study prior to the inauguration of a major project has lived through the anxiety of facing up to management's question, "Why don't we stop right here? What will I learn from the full 2,000 interviews that I haven't learned from these 200?"

What justification does the researcher have for his visceral feeling that to produce findings with anything less than 95 per cent probability is immoral?

In a situation which is constantly changing, it may be far more important to have speed in assessing what is happening than to have accurate and detailed reporting which comes too late to be of more than academic

[4] This is a standard item on the California F-Scales; T. W. Adorno and others, *The Authoritarian Personality* (New York: Harper & Brothers, 1950).

interest. Here the ethos of the researcher as a professional may conflict with his judgments as a businessman.

This is not to say that fast marketing intelligence is at the other end of the pole from conventional marketing surveys. Intelligence, too, must be as systematic as it can be and must adhere to scientific method within the restriction of very limited evidence.

There are three dimensions to intelligence. One is *speed-slowness*. Another is *completeness-incompleteness*. The third is *hardness-softness*. All three of these dimensions set outer limits on the decisions for which intelligence is gathered, regardless of the nature of the problem.

For the military leader, it is of far greater importance to know immediately that the enemy is mounting an offensive than it is to know later the exact middle names of his battalion commanders. And yet what appears to be a complete account of the enemy's battle plan and time schedule may serve no purpose if the source lacks credibility. It takes a nice sense of judgment (call it intuition) to know at what level of hardness or softness information should be taken at face value and should be acted upon.

Something of the same kind of problem confronts every researcher and every user of research, in pondering the relationship between the accuracy of information and its ultimate value.

As an applied art, marketing research is subject to constant pressures to stretch its competence. The researcher is continually being "pushed" by his clients and employers to make his output yield the greatest practical value in terms of generalizations and conclusions. His recommendations may use the actual findings only as a springboard for the researcher's imagination, creative talents, or skills in a field unrelated to research itself.

In fact, his value to clients and employers may be precisely in this secondary realm, rather than in his role as a technician. Imaginative interpretation of research may be condemned as unwarranted inference, or even as distortion. What relevance do solely scientific criteria have to the professional conduct of a practitioner of this type?

INTERPRETATION, CONCLUSION, OR RECOMMENDATION?

If there is a fuzzy distinction between a recommendation and a conclusion, so is there also between an interpretation and a conclusion. An interpretation says, "This is how I would explain the data." A conclusion says, "Here's the real heart of the matter." A recommendation says, "Jump!" or "Stand still!"

There is nothing which may be more dangerous than an uninterpreted set of statistical tables. They can lead a professional, with a knowledge of his subject, off in an entirely different direction from a layman who takes figures too literally or who has no yardstick by which to compare them.

There are many who argue that the researcher should not accede to management's desires for recommendations and suggestions, and that he should confine himself to statements of what he found. Others feel that a researcher should make recommendations, provided that he carefully distinguishes those which he believes to be the conclusions of the research itself from those which stem from his other areas of competence as a marketing specialist.

And there are those who argue that the only thing which really matters is the counsel the researcher can ultimately give his client or employer.

The ultimate user of research normally is not interested in the details of how the researcher came to his final conclusions. He is not too interested either in methodology or in what tests of statistical significance were used. His concern is with what was learned, and what can or should be done about it.

This means that the researcher may be in an excellent position to exercise business judgment, even though he is in no position at all to deliver a professional conclusion.

The researcher in business is often a man in a dilemma, facing both his business loyalties and a set of professional goals which he cannot clearly define.

In this respect, though, the marketing research man has a lot of company. *All professionals* face inconsistencies between means and ends, about goals and values. By understanding our own motivations, by making explicit the contradictions as they occur, we do the most to enhance our professional status, our self-esteem and the productivity of our efforts.

When a researcher is torn between his dual loyalties to his academic discipline and to the pragmatic requirements of his job, he sometimes resolves his dilemma by redefining himself as a practitioner rather than as a scientist. Bernard Berelson moves toward this conclusion as he examines the differences between basic and applied research in the following paper.

His illustrations are drawn from what he describes as "the hardest market research job in the world, as well as the most important one"—the task of coping with the recent dangerous rise in the rate of the world's population growth. Although the substantive problems of this field appear remote from those in which the market researcher conventionally is engaged in his own particular firm, the logic of this approach is a familiar one. The demographer's analysis of vital statistics is, in a way, comparable to the trend analyses of the sales analyst. Attitude surveys of fertility have their analogs in the conventional surveys of consumer preferences and behavior. The action experiments the author describes are like the market tests which accompany new product introductions or shifts in media and copy strategy.

The very magnitude of the problems dealt with by population researchers forces them to be concerned first with solutions and second with pure science. Thus, the researcher who wants to get on with the job is apt to turn into a man of action, an administrator or policy-maker concerned with implementing research findings, and less a scholar concerned with investigating meanings and causes.

Dr. Berelson, formerly vice-president and now President of the Population Council, is an applied social researcher of extraordinarily broad interests. He is a former director of the Bureau of Applied Social Research at Columbia University and has been dean of the Library School and professor of business at the University of Chicago. For a number of years, he served as head of the behavioral sciences for the Ford Foundation. The books he has co-authored include, The People's Choice *and* Human Behavior. *He is a former president of the American Association for Public Opinion Research.*

2. The Researcher as a Man of Action*

BERNARD BERELSON

I believe that the usual rationale for applied sociology is misleading, if not mistaken. What is wrong is to think of applied work primarily as a concomitant of basic academic research—to think of applied work, that is, as a spill-off from a basic study or as a convenient site or subject for fund-raising for a basic inquiry. The result is, more often than not, inappropriate for one or both, discriminatory against one or the other, or diluted for both. The reason is that the basic and the applied are different masters, and it is hard to serve both well simultaneously.

As background, let me mention in shorthand form the condition, the causes, and the consequences of what is known as the "population problem." The condition is undue population growth—currently, the growth rate for the world is just over 2 per cent a year, and in the developing areas of the world is at least 2.5 per cent. At the present rate, today's world population of nearly 3.5 billion will double by the end of the century, and the over 2 billion population of the developing countries will double by 1990. It is literally true that this is a unique situation in human history. Never before has the population grown at anywhere near the rate of the past 20 years. And the enemy is not a number, but a rate.

The cause is to be found not in a higher birth rate, but in a lower death rate—a decline dating essentially from the end of World War II and occurring mainly in the developing countries. The decline is due partly to improved food production and distribution and to a more efficient social organization. But it is perhaps primarily due to the mass application of modern public health measures. As time is figured in such matters, there has been rather sudden application of public health measures that were taken over from the developed countries. In short, the developing countries have successfully imported death control.

However, it is the consequences that are important. The consequences are that some developing countries are having difficulties in feeding their people; that many are becoming dependent upon the importation of food; and that all are being impeded in their efforts to improve standards of living, to insure better health, to spread literacy and education, to secure the bene-

*Presented to the Market Research Council, June 17, 1966.

fits of modern technology—in short, to provide their people with a better way of life. That is, at heart, what the population problem is all about: not about numbers, however striking they may be, but about the quality of human life throughout the world.

What is being done about it? A recent publication, *Family Planning and Population Programs: A Review of World Developments* (University of Chicago Press, 1966, 848 pages), documents the answer in some detail. There are now governmental programs to implement family planning in countries that have over a majority of the population of the developing world. Governments in Asia, Africa, the Middle East, and Latin America have set up formal programs, usually within their ministries of health, and have put substantial government funds into them. There are only six developing countries with populations of 20 million or over that do not have some such formal apparatus set up for population control and family limitation. In Asia, such programs cover something on the order of 70 to 80 per cent of the population, and in Africa and Latin America, about 20 per cent of the population. Programs are expanding almost monthly.

It is fair to say that this is the hardest market research job in the world, as well as the most important one. For after all, the spread of family planning can be seen as a marketing innovation. What we seek is to implement family planning, in countries where it is not now institutionalized, under completely voluntary and free conditions.

As an indication of the magnitude and complexity of the task, let me mention some of the obstacles: illiteracy; ignorance of family planning purposes, means, or consequences; inertia and apathy, resting upon century-old traditions; peasant resistance to change; costs to both the society and the individual; dispersal of population into thousands of small villages; lack of communication between husband and wife with regard to size-of-family considerations; delicacy and intimacy of the subject matter; desire for children or sons for familial, economic, and status reasons (sons being the social security system for old age in such societies); occasional moral, religious, or ideological objections; typical subordination of women, so that the mother's role is essentially the only one open to women; early marriages and high marriage rates, so that virtually the whole of the reproductive capacity of the woman is included within marriage; occasional ineffectiveness of the simpler contraceptive methods and, hence, failure and discouragement at the outset; lack of trained personnel for action programs; little differential fertility as a lever to start with (that is, relatively few small families, except among the better educated classes, mainly in the cities); lack of an adequate system of distribution for contraceptive materials; remote and problematic rewards for successful action, in that it takes two or three years before a couple has a return in a prevented birth for a practice that requires energy and cost on their part; invisibility of social support, deriving from the privacy of the practice (that is, although substantial proportions of women, and men too, in the developing world do want to limit their families, people tend not to know that others are of the same persuasion as themselves, and hence the kind of group reinforcement of the practice that would emerge on a more visible subject is lacking on this one); a limited social organization with which to reach people; and, in many parts of the world, slowly declining mortality rates, so that it takes some time for the typical villager to appreciate the fact that, in order to have a given number of children living till one's own old age, it is no longer necessary to have nearly twice that number born. (Just ask yourself how an illiterate villager in India comes to know that infant mortality is down in his village. We know because we read charts. But how is the Indian villager to understand that his children's generation has a better chance to survive to adulthood than his own generation did? The decline is first perceived, often, as an increase in the number of births in the village, since there are more children around!)

As can be seen from this list, there are tremendous obstacles in practice to institutionalizing an innovation as close to the center of life processes as family planning. This can perhaps be dramatized by the following quotation from my predecessor as President of the Population Council, Dr. Frank W. Notestein, who once drew a parallel between establishing birth control and death control in such societies:

> Consider what would happen if malaria were as welcome as children: If a majority of young couples felt that they really had not justified their existence until they had undergone four or five attacks of malaria, which, moreover, they thoroughly enjoyed; if their fathers, mothers, mothers-in-law, uncles and aunts were constantly urging them to become exposed to this disease as soon as possible; if each new onslaught were welcomed with approbation by the whole community; and if to avoid this attractive disease each deviant couple had to spray its own home with DDT acquired somewhat furtively.

Malaria eradication programs are reasonably successful in the developing countries; but think what difficulties they would face if they were subject to those considerations.

Now, against that background, what is being done by way of research on action programs aimed at implementing birth control in the developing countries? I think it can be said there have been five major kinds of research activities applied in one way or another to such programs.

First, there are economic studies of the relationship between demographic trends and economic growth. A classic in this field is the Coale-Hoover study, *Population Growth and Economic Development in Low Income Countries* (Princeton University Press, 1958), which analyzed the problem India would face if its population continued to grow at the rate current when this study was done in the mid-1950's. This is an economic analysis of the pressures that undue population growth puts upon a society that is struggling to increase its capital investment and to achieve the modern technology that alone can raise the standard of living in a predominantly agricultural society. Such studies have been quite influential with members of economic planning boards.

Second, there is the effort to get good vital statistics. There are very few places in the developing world that have adequate systems of vital statistics in which one can promptly get a measurement of birth rates and changes in birth rates. This is now possible, for example, in Taiwan and Tunisia, but hardly anywhere else. Thus, if one is trying to measure a decline of, say, two or three points in the birth rate, it is very difficult to get reliable measures that would tell with much confidence that a program has achieved a result of that magnitude. Since censuses are difficult and expensive, there have been a number of experimental efforts symbolized by the initials PGE—population growth estimates—that try on a sample survey basis to get some measures of what birth and death rates actually are.

Technicians in this field will appreciate that it is an extremely difficult task to count births and deaths over a recent period. In some efforts now underway, a sample survey is taken in an area and, at the same time, a registrar system is set up there. Someone in the village is paid to keep a record of births and deaths, day by day, and that record is then compared with the findings of the survey. What happens, of course, is that one can match most of these vital events; but there are a number that the registrar picks up and the survey does not, and others that the survey picks up and the registrar does not. If the analyst decides that any event mentioned is a real event and adds them together, he gets one birth rate; but if he follows a different procedure—like taking only events that both methods report—then he gets quite a different rate. I think it is fair to say that we are still in the process of trying to work out ways to get valid birth and death data and that we shall be continuing that effort over the next few years. The importance for evaluational efforts is clear: The first requisite is good vital data.

Third, some studies are of a basic behavioral-science character, being concerned with family structure, kinship patterns, informal communication networks, innovating personality patterns, role relations between men and women, and so on. In my view, such efforts have not substantially contributed to the actual implementation of family planning programs, and little of the current research in the field is of that kind.

Fourth are what we have come to call KAP surveys—the initials stand for knowledge, attitudes, and practices with regard to fertility. In the past five years or so, there have been about 20 KAP surveys done in a quite proficient way in that many countries throughout the world. So we now have material on the following: knowledge of the physiology of reproduction and of contraceptive methods; attitudes on use of contraception, on family size, on governmental programs, and the like; and data on the actual practice of family planning. This is one of the most substantial, internationally comparable sets of data on an important social question that now exists. And more such studies are in progress. A KAP survey done at the outset of a program and repeated later is a good way to get some feedback on how well the program is doing and what it is actually accomplishing. Such evaluations are now under way.

Fifth and finally, there are direct evaluations of action experiments, conducted under quite realistic conditions. The field has progressed to the point where we can do this on a large scale now. For example, one of the major and most elaborate efforts was carried on in Taichung, Taiwan, a city of 300,000 population, where among other things we learned that there is a good deal of diffusion on this matter so that size of population provides a critical mass phenomenon that one can exploit. Of the studies done with the purpose of making the action program more efficient, the most successful, to my mind, have been quick, focussed studies to test out an idea that might be viable in the larger program.

For example, in Taiwan, the normal charge for an IUD insertion (short for the new intrauterine device) is $1.50, with the patient paying half and the national program paying the other half, on a coupon-fee basis. Typically in this program, paid workers go into the field in order to inform women about the program and distribute coupons to be turned in to the nearby doctor. But someone said, "Suppose you had a free offer for a limited time only, and anybody who wants the IUD can save 75 cents if the coupon is redeemed by a certain date. Would the savings to the program in field workers be offset by the extra cost of insertion? What would happen to acceptances?" That presents a neat little experimental situation, and the Taiwanese did a study of that sort with a control area. They kept careful records on costs and were able to tell the administrator what the differential returns were for considering possible institutionalization in the national program.

As another example, they studied what would happen if instead of simply giving a coupon to the woman and telling her the location of the participating doctors, they gave the interested woman an actual appointment at a specific time. Here again, they could soon show what difference that made. Or again, they experimented with distributing coupons through people whose normal duties brought them into contact with large numbers of other people—for example, door-to-door salesmen, hairdressers, barbers, and so on. Such people received a small referral fee when their coupons were turned in, and the obvious economic records were kept to check on relative return from such an effort as compared with the regular full-time field workers. Or again, does the program have to hold group meetings in every neighborhood, or will they be nearly as effective in every 2nd or 3rd or 5th one? This is one of the ways we have learned that this innovation, which turns out to be a popular one, has a great deal of diffusion effect built into it, and we are beginning to get a sense of what the diffusion patterns are.

Finally, take an example from another country. In Tunisia, the political party is certainly one of the best communication networks down to the grassroots. The President was so interested in the success of this program that he authorized the party to carry the message down to the men in the villages. Information and education are flowing through that network, and the experimental districts have a much better record of acceptances.

The key point is that such studies can be done—they can be done well, they can be done quickly, and they can be done with the resources normally available in the national program so that they can be incorporated therein if the results warrant. That is their great virtue. Major program guidance in the large-scale efforts has come, I think, from such targeted, operational studies.

The limitations of research are indicated by the major ingredients of a successful program to implement family planning in a developing country. They are three.

First is the need for a good contraceptive technology. Happily, with the oral pill and the new IUD, we are now in a much better position than we were in only a few years ago. If we were still dependent on the conventional contraceptive methods, such programs would not have been nearly as successful as they are with the IUD's.

Second, there must be interest or motivation on the part of the people. I have found it useful never to talk about interest without also talking about technology, because these two factors are so closely interrelated. If one has an easy contraceptive method, then at any given level of interest you can get much more acceptance; if one has a hard contraceptive method, then it is only the highly motivated who will be available. To the extent that the technology improves, then, the program can be effective much further down the scale of interest. I personally believe that, for the visible future, the likely improvements in contraceptive technology will be more effective in spreading acceptance in the developing countries than the likely increases in individual motivation and interest. Particularly in the short run of, for example, three to five years, technology promises the larger returns.

Third, organization is needed to bring the technology to the interest. This is where the programs need improvement—in administrative capacity, in the skills of organizing and doing something, in lessening bureaucratic restrictions, and so on.

All of the preceding ties into some large considerations on how to go about applied social research of this kind.* Let me quickly indicate some differences between what seem to me to be the wrong and right ways to go about social research on action programs—that is, differences that are associated with having an impact on the problem presented, assuming that this is the objective:

> The wrong way to go about applied social research tends to concentrate on contributing to the theory or the techniques of discipline; the

*I borrow here from my article in Arthur B. Shostak, ed., *Sociology In Action: Case Studies in Social Problems and Directed Social Change;* Dorsey Press, 1966.

right way concentrates on contributing to the solution or amelioration of a problem.

The former insists on sticking with pure research; the latter is willing to move outside research into action or administration in order to follow the problem to a satisfactory conclusion.

The former seeks generalizations and hopes the present case can be guided thereby; the latter is prepared to stick to the individual case, and work out from there.

The former tends to go for basic processes; the latter goes for what might make a desired difference, however superficial it may be.

The former is after the *why*; the latter is after the *how*.

The former mainly requires technical judgments; the latter requires, in addition, a sense of what the situation and the personalities will bear, what the economics will support, how much change can be introduced, and how quickly—in short, it requires mature administrative judgment as well as technical proficiency.

The former is content with small differences, if statistically sound; the latter appreciates that the administrator cannot typically deal with small differences secured through sophisticated analyses of tiny subsamples and, thus, is looking for the main lines of action—for important differences, not just significant ones.

The former typically seeks the facts on the assumption that they will point automatically to action; the latter proceeds on the principle that, for action purposes, the researcher should collect no facts unless they speak reasonably directly to an administrative decision, to actionable alternatives usually recognized in advance.

The former aims at publishing a research report, preferably a book, which in major studies will appear about five years after the field work is done, if then; the latter is content with a memorandum, or a series thereof, bringing out the main actionable points quickly.

The former usually reports in the technical language of the discipline; the latter tends to report in the common language, since that is where the decisions will also be stated. The one, in short, aims at coming to conclusions; the other aims at reaching decisions—and the two are not the same.

I deliberately sharpen the case here in order to make the point, as clearly as possible, that there are major differences between what usually passes as applied social research and what could happen if we were more self-conscious about what we are trying to do.

What this comes down to is a big issue indeed. For what is implicit in these differences is the distinction between an academic discipline and a profession; and what I am saying is that applied work in this field should be modeled more on the latter than the former. Professions are based on academic disciplines, but they are by no means the same. Professions deal with individual cases; they are after practical consequences that matter; their first allegiance is the treatment of the particular case; they must make decisions despite uncertainty.

Has the time come for the emergence of a profession out of the behavioral sciences, as with the relation of medicine to biology, engineering to physics, and the business schools to economics? My own answer is "Yes," to a limited degree—limited because we still have few self-conscious and self-respecting practitioners of this type and because the idea needs slow and careful development. In some ways we are on the road, but only partially so. What I like to call policy research, in the sense presented here, is certainly coming. If nothing else, the demands of the complex mass society will call forth such applied studies in education, law, health, art and culture, the mass media, urban affairs, crime and delinquency, and, to return to where we started, population control.

PART TWO

Researcher and Respondent

The quality of research data, the conclusions drawn by the research, and the action taken by clients on the basis of research information—none of these can be any better than the level of confidence which the public at large has in survey research. Public willingness to cooperate in interviews is threatened by the practice of sales solicitations made in the guise of legitimate surveys. In the following paper, Richard Baxter suggests that the problem is big and getting bigger, but that there are ways of coping with it through effective action on the part of the research community.

Dr. Baxter, a sociologist by training, conducted research for the U.S. Information Agency and for Columbia University's Bureau of Applied Social Research before entering the business world. He has been vice-president of research for Cunningham and Walsh, director of planning and research for the Associated Merchandising Corporation, and currently is Vice-President and Director of Research Services for Benton and Bowles. He is President of the Market Research Council, 1968–69.

3. The Harassed Respondent: I. Sales Solicitation in the Guise of Consumer Research*

RICHARD BAXTER

The telephone rings, and you answer. A voice says, "Hello, this is ______ calling, of (an ambiguously descriptive firm name). I am conducting a study dealing with the ______ market. I would like to ask you just a few questions which will only take a minute or two." A series of questions are then asked which obtain specific data on certain big ticket items currently owned in the household. If certain models are owned, the interviewer then asks whether the item was purchased *new* or *used* and what the family's buying intentions are for a new model. (If the last item purchased was *used,* the interview is terminated.)

So far so good. To this point, the respondent is being surveyed in a buying-intention study.

But then what happens? On the back of the questionnaires are instructions to the interviewers, including a sample form which the interviewer is given to fill out for each respondent contacted. The interviewer is given a batch of these forms. In addition to pre-codes for circling by the interviewer, indicating the time of the respondent's intended purchase of the product, are the following items: "Salesman's Name," "Date of Sale," "Name of Retail Outlet." The next item reads, "When the sale and delivery of ______ has been made to the prospect listed above, complete the required information and submit this report of sale to your dealer for approval and forwarding to the (manufacturer's District Office)."

A watch company sends out sale promotional material and a questionnaire. One side of the post-card size questionnaire has a few rudimentary questions on media preferences and preferred retail outlet for watch purchasing. The other side is an order form which the respondent can fill out after having read through a color brochure illustrating and describing various watch models.

---

*Presented to the Market Research Council, September 17, 1965.

A gasoline company uses the name "Research Center" as the return address for a credit-card solicitation.

A mailing house sends questionnaires by mail to develop mailing lists, with the promise that people who fill out the questionnaires will have the opportunity to win "fabulous gifts." When queried about the purpose of the questionnaire, a form letter came back from the firm indicating that the purpose was to "enable us to do a better job of selecting names from our overall list for particular mailings." This form letter also was sent to recipients of the questionnaire who wrote the mailing house to learn more about the project.

Millions of American households have been approached—by mail, by telephone, and in person—by usurpers of legitimate research techniques, for the purpose of making sales.

Once, while I was associated with an advertising agency, a subsidiary of a well-known market research firm asked for an appointment with one of the agency's marketing executives. At a subsequent hour and a half meeting, three were present: the agency marketing man, the sales representative from the outside firm, and I. (I was *not* identified as a researcher). The essence of this firm's offer was to obtain and provide to us the names and addresses of prospects for residential air conditioners. It was made clear that these prospects would be approached as in a market research survey and that they would not know that their names were to be turned over as sales leads.

Marketing and sales executives of manufacturing companies, of advertising agencies, and of other kinds of business institutions are being solicited increasingly—either in person or by mail—by firms that offer their services to obtain the names of customer prospects for products and services. These names are then made available to the client organization. This, of course, is a legitimate activity, provided there is no implication to the prospective customer that he has been interviewed in an opinion or market survey.

The researcher's complaint is that the survey approach frequently is misused to obtain sales leads for later use or to attempt to sell something to the respondent during the course of the interview. Such unethical practices are not easy to control. Cases have been noted, for example, in which the sales solicitor interviewing to identify prospects *departs* from a script that would have been acceptable to the researcher because it did not camouflage the true purpose of the sales call. There is no assurance that an ethically clean sales-canvass script will not be converted into a deceptive survey-approach in actual field use.

It has long been a practice in industrial market research, particularly in studies of market potentials for new products in the big ticket industrial product field, for the names of respondents to be turned over to sales staffs of the client company. This very point, in fact, was about the only bone of contention within the American Marketing Association Ethics Committee when we developed a Code of Ethics three or four years ago. This Code was approved overwhelmingly by the members of the AMA, but there was a vociferous minority which felt we were being unrealistic by insisting on the anonymity of respondents in market research surveys. I know that some experienced, industrial market researchers felt that our committee members were "nice nellies." But we do have reason to be concerned about an apparently increasing misuse of the survey technique by sales canvassers. There are two reasons for this concern.

The first is that public confusion, annoyance, and distrust of field interviewers over a few years, resulting from unfortunate experiences with deceptive "survey" practices, can seriously impede legitimate survey activity. We have a reservoir of public good will to protect. That good will really keeps us in business. It is the *essential* raw material from which opinion and market research is made. We shouldn't jeopardize the public's willingness to submit to interviews.

The second reason we are concerned is that more and more states and local governments are attempting to regulate or restrict bona-fide market and opinion survey interviewing, and there are signs that interviewers are being classified—in the minds of many public authorities—along with peddlers.

Let's look at each of these points. Elmo Roper and Associates included a question series in a nationwide survey that was conducted in May, 1963 (using an area probability sample of 3,919 cases). The first question was: "Has anyone ever said he wanted to interview you on a survey—either in person or by telephone, and then tried to sell you something?"

The percentages who answered "Yes" were:

	Total	*Men*	*Women*
	27%	25%	30%
100% =	(3,919)	(1,957)	(1,962)

Note that about one-fourth of adults in the United States believe that they have been approached on a "survey" whose real purpose was to sell the respondent something—with somewhat more women than men reporting such an experience.

The table on page 26 presents some figures on the kinds of products and services which were the subjects of these "deceptive surveys."

The following is a press release from the Opinion Research Corporation, dated October 21, 1964:

> PRINCETON, N.J.—Almost as many persons are being asked for interviews by salesmen posing as "interviewers" as by legitimate interviewers for survey organizations, a study by Opinion Research Corporation has found.
>
> A nationwide probability sample of 2,035 adults participated in the research.
>
> Almost one person in four (24%) said he had been approached

Subject of "Deceptive Surveys"	%
Magazines	28
Books, encylopedias	26
Screens, storm windows	10
Electrical appliances (other than vacuum cleaners)	9
Vacuum cleaners	7
Insurance	7
Photographs, pictures	6
Lessons—dance, piano, etc.	3
Sidings	3
Household sundries	2
Cosmetics, toiletries	1
Cars	1
All other	12
Don't know or no answer	10
	100% = (1,061)

at some time by someone who claimed to be an interviewer and turned out to be a salesman using a survey as a device to get one foot in the door.

On the other hand, some 29 per cent of participants in the ORC study, a slightly larger proportion, reported they had been interviewed previously by legitimate research firms.

Joseph C. Bevis, ORC Chairman, said the findings reflected a serious problem for research organizations and the clients they serve. "The public's willingness to participate in research is based largely on good will and appreciation of the importance of such efforts," he said. "When surveys are misrepresented and the public is misled, obtaining the cooperation essential to effective research becomes increasingly difficult."

Of participants who said they had been approached by phony interviewers, 30 per cent reported the salesman's product was a magazine and 25 per cent said the product was an encyclopedia.

Eighteen different magazines and eleven different encyclopedias were cited.

Some 52 other products and services also were cited including brassieres, dancing lessons, TV sets, freezers, and cemetery lots.

There is, then, convincing evidence of the abuse of public good will by sales canvassers using the survey technique to gain entry or information at the respondent's doorstep or telephone mouthpiece.

What has been the measurable effect of all this deception on getting interviews? The survey evidence we have does *not* show an increase in the interview refusal rate in legitimate market and opinion surveys. At least, we had not found an increase up to 1963. In that year, the Public Relations Committee of the American Association for Public Opinion Research sent letters to certain individual members of AAPOR who also are principals of research organizations. Twenty-six persons replied. Fifteen of the 26 organizations represented have field interviewing activity. This was not a representative sample of U.S. research organizations, but I think the results can be used to illustrate the opinions held by many professional researchers concerning this problem.

By a ratio of about two to one, more survey practitioners expressed the opinion that refusal rates are *not* a problem, or are not increasing, than expressed the opinion that refusals *are* a problem or are increasing. Those who did see a refusal problem were asked what was causing it, in their opinion. Undoubtedly cued to some extent by the content of the inquiry we sent them, more of the researchers mentioned mistrust of market researchers by people refusing to be interviewed than any other reason. It is evident that there is some concern in our professional fraternity concerning this problem. Many of those replying to the AAPOR Committee gave examples of how fraudulent use of the survey approach has impaired legitimate survey research activity. The tenor of this problem is much easier to understand through exposure to actual field cases than by reading statistics on the incidence of deception involving the survey technique.

1. In 1963, in a Texas town, a telephone interview survey on coffee was conducted, involving a sample of 440 women. Only 380 of these interviews could be completed—a 13.6 per cent refusal rate. This rate is sharply above that found in 16 other cities in which the identical interview approach was used. The normal rate of refusal was under 2 per cent, which also had been the rate for two previous studies in the same town, using the very same interview questions.

   Because of this discrepancy in refusal rates, refusals were analyzed. It was found that a telephone canvass had been conducted in that area about three weeks before this survey. The earlier canvass actually was for sales purposes, and involved the use of a market research telephone survey approach to obtain names of customer prospects for use by local dealers of the company that authorized the canvass. Suspicion of all market studies was cited by respondents who refused to be interviewed in the later bona-fide market and opinion research survey.
2. Another survey operator we contacted referred to a survey conducted in the spring of 1963 in which four out of five eligible respondents interviewed by telephone refused a personal interview that was to follow, largely because of their fear of a later sales effort.

   Boston, Providence, and "probably other markets" caused trouble to another of our responding research firms, which was attributed to an earlier automotive survey.

   Still another survey practitioner said: "The types of studies which seem to run into more closed doors usually involve magazine readership —also—a degree of difficulty on studies (of) baby care products, and with frozen food surveys. The reason is easily traceable to the fact that magazine and book salesmen, diaper services and freezer plan salesmen make a great deal of use out of the public opinion interview as a means of obtaining leads for further sales."

What about the second reason for our fear concerning the abuse of legitimate survey research? The latest statistics I have show that about 250 communities in 34 states have some kind of restrictions on field interviewing for surveys. This is not necessarily bad. Legitimate interviewers can be protected, in effect, by ordinances attempting to screen and control various kinds of approaches made to the public. But the nature of a large share of this local regulation is undoubtedly restrictive, causing additional field problems and expense. The following are some examples.

According to information received from operating research organizations whom we contacted, no interviewing whatever is allowed in the California cities of Arcadia, Beverly Hills, San Marino, and Huntingdon Beach, and in other scattered communities, for example, one or two well-to-do suburbs of Miami. Licenses are required in Burbank, Pico Rivera, South Pasedena, Chula Vista, and La Mesa, in California. Burbank charges $50, South Pasedena $20. In some of the Chicago areas $5 or $10 is charged, and in some cases every time—that is, each day—that the locale is used. In some communities no evening or weekend interviewing is allowed. The research organizations we corresponded with tell us that there are increasing restrictions and intervention by suburban township authorities and questioning by police.

What does all this mean? Many of us believe that the evidence is clear that respondents are being abused by deceptive market and opinion "surveyers." We believe that continued activity of this kind is endangering the reservoir of public good will, and also will have an effect on regulatory and legislative officials in states and local communities.

What can we do about it?

1. If you or a member of your family is approached as a respondent in a deceptive "survey," get details, such as the name and address of the interviewing or sales canvassing organization, the name of the "interviewer," the time and date of the interview, the nature of the survey, product, or service categories being studied, a copy of the questionnaire. Send this information to the Standards Committee of organizations like the American Association for Public Opinion Research or the American Marketing Association which have Codes of proper practice and which should be prepared to look into the matter.
2. If you are a research professional in the field, you, your firm, or other professionals you know might be approached by a prospective client who wants a "sales lead" job done, using the survey research method. Such approaches should also be brought to the attention of one of the

professional organizations. The American Association for Public Opinion Research recently changed from a loosely organized association of individuals to a corporation—with the express purpose of taking action to stop misuse of the survey technique. Prior to this incorporation, there were legal barriers to effective action. The organization already has moved to stop some deceptive practices.

3. For added pressure from an important agency in the area of deceptive business practices, notify the National Better Business Bureau in New York, if the offending "survey" sponsor is a national or regional firm that you suspect is operating in more than one community. The Bureau has taken effective action on past abuses.
4. Encourage the use by interviewers of the National Better Business Bureau's "Memo to the Public"—or whatever similar form is most effective in a given community (it may be a form by a local Chamber of Commerce or municipal bureau). Such instruments *cannot* be used by the phony interviewer without the danger of a "boomerang effect" on his company's sales effort, because these memos *assure,* in print, that no sales effort will be made.
5. Every research organization should consider the development of a public information program. It need not be expensive, nor complicated. Try to get interviewing supervisors employed by your firm on programs of service and civic clubs, women's organizations, and the like, to explain the value of true market and opinion research in their communities. Your staff people could write up a sample script for such a speech.

   The Opinion Research Corporation, for example, made up a kit of materials about two and a half years ago which was distributed to newspapers in some 400 communities for use in feature stories about interviewing, about particular interviewers, and about bona-fide survey research. A very satisfactory proportion of papers did use the materials. ORC also determined which of its interviewers would be willing to be interviewed on local radio and television stations and in newspapers, and then ORC notified the local media of the availability of these interviewers. There are hundreds, probably thousands, of "interview programs" on local stations across the country which are continually looking for interesting program material and personalities.

Our profession needs authoritative action to stop unethical and damaging pseudo-research activity. But this action can be taken only if individuals call infractions to the attention of appropriate professional organizations. The time has already gone by when we can sit by and "let George do it."

The central body of data in marketing research stems from consumer surveys. At the heart of the survey method itself lies an unspoken covenant between interviewer and respondent. To the interviewer, respondents give freely of their time and of their private thoughts. The only expectation of reward is the fun of being interviewed itself and the slight lift to the respondent's self-esteem. He may have a vague hope that better information on the part of the powers that be will somehow improve the excellence of the judgments that are made in putting products on the market, or TV programs on the air.

Implicit in this covenant is the assumption that the respondent's words, though interesting and important in their own right, will ultimately be lost and anonymous in a sea of numbers, that they represent only a part of the total array of statistical data being collected, and that the individual cannot be identified or suffer any harmful consequences as a result of the interview.

As in any interpersonal relationship, the contact of respondent and interviewer raises questions of ethics. It is to these moral questions that Robert Carlson addresses himself in the next paper. Carlson sees the question of privacy in survey research as part of the larger moral problem which social scientists confront when they use human beings as subjects (and therefore as "objects"). In this respect, the interviewer talking to a respondent in a marketing survey is but a step removed from the experimental psychologist who places human guinea pigs in simulated stress situations in a laboratory.

The author raises the intriguing suggestion that since practitioners of research owe a debt to the society which so freely provides them with data, they can best repay this debt by putting their skills to work voluntarily on matters of social consequence. Dr. Carlson, a former president of the American Association for Public Opinion Research, is a sociologist who has worked for the U.S. Public Health Service and for the Columbia University Bureau of Applied Social Research. He is advisor on overseas public relations for the Standard Oil Company (New Jersey).

4. The Issue of Privacy in Public Opinion Research*

ROBERT O. CARLSON

In this paper I shall view with some alarm the short-term prospects of public opinion research as it relates to the issue of privacy. I believe it is a real issue and that, by the very nature of public opinion work, we must invade the privacy of our respondents in some measure. I feel this invasion can be justified, but unfortunately we have done a poor job up to now of explaining ourselves and our work to our publics.

Things have been going along rather too well for us as a profession, except for an occasional effort to legislate against door-to-door interviewing on a municipal or state level, as well as some scattered instances of pseudo-surveys being used for selling merchandise. This experience compares favorably with the harassment and the investigations which those in the field of psychological testing have undergone. I am concerned that we in the survey research field underestimate the likelihood of our activities facing similar scrutiny and public controversy. As a thriving new profession, exercising considerable power in government, academic, and business circles, it is unrealistic to expect that we can escape the searching eye of critics and the general public with respect to the issue of privacy and the work we do.

Some of us seem to operate on the bland assumption that the issue of privacy has little or no relevance for the field of public opinion research. In its most extreme form, this view is reflected in the philosophy that we as researchers have the right to ask people their opinions on a broad range of questions and they, in turn, have the right to answer or to refuse to answer our questions. Let us pause at this juncture and give a little more thought to this beguiling and comforting proposition. However, let us view it from the point of view of a potential critic who turns the tables on us and begins to ask us some questions about the basic tool of our trade—the interview.

For example, what is our answer to the critic who may say, "The people you interview in your surveys are not all alike. Some are well educated, have a high socio-economic status, are intellectually and psychologically

*Reprinted from *Public Opinion Quarterly*, Vol. XXXI, No. 1 (Spring, 1967), pp. 1–8. This paper was originally presented to the American Association for Public Opinion Research, May 6, 1966.

secure and sophisticated, and these, of course, can be expected to know that they do not have to answer the questions your interviewers bring to their homes. But," continues our critic, "what of the others in the population who are old, poor, badly educated members of ethnic groups who harbor fear of authority figures from the outside world and a host of similar categories—are these people equally aware of their right not to answer your questions and are they equally prepared psychologically to exercise this right?" I do not think we have adequate answers to this question, and yet answers would be of considerable interest to us from a purely research standpoint, quite apart from the light such data might shed on the privacy question itself. Why should not the appendix of each opinion survey give the available characteristics of the people who refused to be interviewed as well as those who participated in a survey?

Clearly, the interview situation in a typical public opinion survey is the point at which the privacy issue takes on its greatest meaning. It dramatizes the dilemma of where the rights of the individual leave off and the needs of our society for better scientific information on human behavior take over. It would be naïve and even amusing for me to suggest that interviewers should preface their questions with a reminder to a potential respondent that he has a right not to be interviewed. However amusing and ingenuous this idea may seem, I remind you that our psychological colleagues are very much concerned about it. Many of their leading spokesmen have stated that every individual should be informed that he is free to participate or not in any particular psychological test before it is administered to him.

But there are still other aspects of the interview situation that our critics might insist represent an invasion of the privacy of respondents, and we do well to consider these matters. For example, an interviewer may gain access to a home by indicating in vague terms the nature of the survey he is conducting. Once having been admitted and having established rapport with his informant, the interviewer is free to move from his relatively innocuous initial questions into subject areas of a highly personal nature—posing questions having to do with the political, religious, economic, and moral beliefs and practices of the respondent. Such questions no doubt are essential for many of the surveys we conduct, but they also are capable of generating resistance and resentment. In such instances, does the average respondent realize that he has the right to break off the questioning any time he may wish, even though he has given his earlier agreement to participate in the survey? This rhetorical question merely illustrates one of the many aspects about the interview situation on which we have far too little data. True, there are countless articles on how to win rapport, how to phrase questions, how to probe for more complete answers, how to assess interviewer bias, and so forth—but we have uncommonly few descriptions of the interview as a real life power situation in which both the respondent and the interviewer play out their separate and often conflicting roles. Central to any such discussion of the interview as a social phenomenon would be a consideration of how much the respondent knows about his rights vis-à-vis the interviewer. Such a study would be a splendid addition to the standard textbook, *Interviewing in Social Research,* by Hyman and his associates at NORC.*

Still another related aspect of the privacy issue in survey research work arises when the respondent is asked to report on the actions, attitudes, beliefs, and behavior of his family, his neighbors, his fellow workers, and others who are in close association with him. To what extent do we in the research fraternity run the risk of being seen as professional snoopers and private CIA agents when we employ such questions? Once again, one can see the potential conflict between our valid need for this kind of information in understanding aspects of human behavior and the equally salient concern which the public has that the research process may be abused or misused.

On another score we face a similar moral dilemma. Today there is widespread concern over the extensive use of electronic devices to spy on the most private aspects of our lives. Whether the gadgets are hidden cameras or microphones or tape recorders, they have in common the aim of causing people to reveal things about their lives that they would be most reluctant to reveal of their own free will. With this widespread concern being expressed in the press and in legislative halls, is it possible that we will be criticized for planting projective questions in our interview schedules and thereby psychologically bugging the minds of our respondents and causing them to reveal information about themselves that they otherwise would not? Far-fetched and ludicrous, you say? Perhaps, but it can be argued that when we use projective questions in a general opinion survey, we are employing the tools of the clinical psychologist without always ensuring that the same controls are imposed on the use and analysis of these projective questions that the psychologist imposes with his clients.

Of course, one of the most common means of gaining electronic entry to a home is the telephone. Because it is a relatively quick, inexpensive, and convenient research tool (particularly when we are trying to locate certain kinds of respondents from a much larger universe), we all have a stake in encouraging a responsible use of the telephone in survey research. The several telephone companies, interestingly enough, do not feel that this is part of their responsibility. At any rate, it is safe to assume the average telephone subscriber does not see himself as just another potential sampling point in one of our surveys. He pays a monthly rental for his phone and usually has a proprietary feeling about it. The day may come when he reacts to increasing sales solicitations and public opinion surveys by asking why he should help subsidize the research and sales activities of others. There is agitation in some sectors of our country to have phone books indicate by a symbol whether or not the subscriber is willing to cooperate in surveys and sales pitches, and this movement could profoundly affect us.

Still another aspect of the privacy issue is raised when we find it necessary to ask respondents questions about topics that may induce considerable stress and anxiety in their minds—questions having to do with their health

*National Opinion Research Center (at the University of Chicago).

or their level of information on diseases such as cancer, or questions on the likelihood of an atomic war or the possibility of a depression. Once these issues have been raised to the surface of a respondent's mind, they may cause him worry and upset long after the interviewer has said goodbye. In most test situations set up by psychologists, provisions are made for some form of psychic support and therapeutic reassurance to be given to respondents after they have been exposed to anxiety-producing questions. Is it totally unrealistic to have our interviewers give some written or oral reassurance to a respondent at the end of an interview when the subject matter of the survey has dealt with an anxiety-provoking issue?

Finally, on the matter of privacy, there are those standard questions one finds at the end of most surveys dealing with the age, sex, socioeconomic status, education, race, and often the political and religious affiliation of the respondent. It is ironic that we have come to refer to these as census-type questions, inasmuch as the Bureau of the Census has the greatest difficulty in getting approval for collecting data on some of these attributes, even when it can prove that it has an elaborate mechanism for protecting the confidential nature of its data.

The issue in this case is not only our right as researchers to collect such data but, more important, our discretion and maturity of judgment in using them in reporting on the attitudes and the behavior of subgroups in our samples which might be identified and damaged by such revelations. Frankly, I am surprised that we have not felt greater pressure from the various action groups organized to protect the rights of minority groups, regarding our practice of categorizing and reporting on subgroups in our samples. In theory, it can be argued that any subgroup that can be identified by data in a survey report has had its privacy invaded. While I personally would be inclined to reject such reasoning as specious and misguided, I feel we cannot dismiss the possibility of this developing into an important issue at some future date.

In summary, then, the first part of this paper has belabored the proposition that the issue of privacy in public opinion research is a very real one, and that it manifests itself in a wide variety of ways, but most particularly in the interview situation. It may also obtain when we use sloppy procedures in screening, hiring, and supervising coders, typists, clerical personnel, and all other employees who have access to personal data collected in our opinion surveys.

If you grant that we do indeed invade the privacy of our respondents in some measure in the work we do, then I think you might also agree that it becomes important for us to ensure that the public understands why we need this kind of information and why we can be trusted with it. Stated bluntly, the issue of privacy then is linked to the question: What does the public get for permitting us to enter their homes, use up their leisure time, and often explore very private nooks and crannies of their lives? The psychological tester in industry or government can point to a number of direct benefits to the individual, his family, and his society from the various psychological tests he administers. What gratifications and rewards do we offer respondents who take part in our public opinion surveys?

The first and most obvious is that we provide a sympathetic ear to them and offer them a way of getting problems and opinions off their chests. Moreover, respondents probably have their self-esteem enhanced when they are asked opinions on important problems of the day. But, alas, there are also many instances in which the subject matter of a survey is pretty dull and trivial and of interest only to the sponsoring client. What do the respondent and his society get from cooperating with such data-gathering efforts?

Analogies may be misleading and misplaced, and yet I feel it is appropriate to use one in discussing this question and its broader implications. Let's face it, we are able to collect our research data only because the general public continues to be willing to submit to our interviews. This acceptance of us by the public is the basic natural resource on which our industry is built. Without it, we would be out of business tomorrow. Other industries also have been built on the exploitation of other kinds of natural resources—our forests, farmlands, and mines—and it is instructive to remember that during the nineteenth century in this country many of these industries made two errors that in time caused public outcry and pressure on government to regulate them. First, they assumed that the public was not interested in what they were doing and so made no serious effort to explain the contributions they were making to society. Second, they failed to find a mechanism to police a certain few of their members who did not serve the public well.

To date, we in the opinion research business have done a poor job of informing the public about the work we do and the benefits it brings to them. On the other hand, we have formulated a sound code of ethics. Unfortunately, we have only informal means by which to enforce these standards and it may be unrealistic to expect that we will ever be able to do more. Those in our business who most frequently do violence to our standards usually do not belong to professional associations and do not respond readily to informal pressures.

What is the story we should be telling about public opinion research and the benefits the public derives from it? The substance of this message will obviously vary, depending on the type of organization that sponsors public opinion research. Broadly speaking, there are three kinds of clients who commission most public opinion research studies. They are (1) the government, (2) academic and quasiacademic research institutes, usually operating on a nonprofit basis, and (3) commercial research firms, usually trying to operate on a profit basis and fortunately succeeding.

I suspect that each of these three groups has a different degree of acceptance from the public. In the case of government-sponsored research, a certain amount is actually required by law, the best example being the census. But even when not required by law, studies sponsored by government agencies, both Federal and state, seem to have general acceptance—

particularly those dealing with problems in the field of agriculture, health, education, and public welfare. The research work done by these government bureaus has earned high recognition from scholars as well as the general public. In speculating on the degree of acceptance by the public of government-sponsored research, it should be noted that the public ultimately exercises control over these studies through their elected officials, who can authorize greater or less government research effort. Yet, ironically enough, it is in government today that the use of psychological tests is most widely being called into question by congressional critics and others. Is our turn next? Perhaps now is the time for an educational effort to be undertaken with key members of Congress to explain the role public opinion surveys can play in ensuring better planning by government agencies.

It is difficult to speculate on how much the public is aware of the research being carried out by academic and nonprofit research institutes. I suspect there may be times when the recondite nature of their studies may puzzle the public, but I find no evidence that any appreciable number of people question either the motives or the integrity of these research organizations. I assume most of you would agree that a persuasive case can be made for the benefits that the general public derives from these studies. Once more, however, I find myself generally unimpressed by the quality of the reporting these groups do in telling their story to the non–research-oriented world. Their annual reports, when they elect to publish them, are often pedestrian and dull, apparently assigned to a staff writer, and failing altogether to catch the excitement and significance of the problems on which these institutes are working.

Finally, there is the vast field of commercial research, which is designed to help a client improve his market position or his corporate acceptance. These projects are sometimes treated in a pejorative and patronizing way by those who do not know the rigorous technical standards and the imaginative research designs employed in many of these studies. One frequent justification for the social utility of commercial research is that it permits the public to communicate its likes and dislikes to the companies that manufacture our consumer products; produce our newspapers, television programs, and magazines; and provide a host of other consumer services. We in the research business generally assume this function is perfectly obvious to the general public, but I doubt this.

But telling the story of the contributions public opinion research makes to improving the consumer's products must be done with skill. It would be unwise, for example, to use the old cliché that the public is the real boss of the marketplace and that by asking for its opinion about various consumer products we bring democracy to the councils of the business world. One example of where this theme could come back to haunt us is the automotive industry, which has carried out countless consumer surveys. These surveys may or may not have been a factor in causing manufacturers to put chrome and tailfins on their cars instead of building greater safety into them. But the auto industry, and every other industrial consumer of opinion research data, should make it clear that they employ survey research data merely as one among several sources of information that influence their decisions on product design and changes. Thus, opinion surveys provide the consumer with a forum from which he may speak to management, but they do not guarantee him a seat in the board of directors' room.

Candor requires that we also admit that not all commercial surveys have direct social value to our society. Putting aside the question of whether or not cigarette smoking is harmful to health, it just is plain difficult to see how the public benefits when a client commissions a survey designed to learn why the public prefers Brand X to Brand Y. In such cases, the argument I would offer on behalf of the social value of commercial research is that it frequently helps perfect research techniques that can be applied to problems of greater social importance, provided these new research techniques are made available to the world of research scholars. The Roper Public Opinion Research Center at Williams College represented a pioneer effort in the direction of making such data available, and the newly created Council of Social Science Data Archives consolidates the resources of the Roper Center with those of seven other libraries of public opinion research data. Even so, only a small fraction of the research carried out for private industry ever finds its way into those archives or the public domain.

The time has come, in my opinion, for those of us who earn a livelihood from public opinion research to consider how we might make a more concrete contribution to our society. As a very tentative and inadequate first step in this direction, I suggest that the individual firms (or a consortium of some of our larger commercial and academic research groups) donate several public service surveys each year on subjects of importance to the people of the United States. There are endless topics crying out for such study, and some do not have sponsors with money enough to commission such research.

I have discussed at some length our less than excellent public relations position because I think our profession has the resources and reasons to improve it. This job should be undertaken at once, not alone to forestall government interference and regulation of our work, and not alone to protect the dollar investment and the professional commitment that we have in the field of public opinion surveys, but also because a better understanding of our work could very conceivably improve the quality of the data we get from the public. Once we accept the fact that the question of "privacy" is relevant for us in the public opinion research field, I am convinced we can justify our activities and demonstrate their social worth.

As marketing continues to grow as a field of practice, its needs for information steadily increase and the use of survey research becomes more and more widespread. This in turn increases the number of contacts between survey practitioners and the general public, as well as the probability that any given person will be interviewed.

The next paper takes up a number of the conditions which might give respondents a sense of harassment and discourage their cooperation in surveys. Paul Sheatsley, an authority on the methodology of interviewing and field research practices, is less perturbed about the state of respondent cooperation than are some of the other contributors to this symposium. He suggests that harassment can be defined essentially by subjective criteria and that project directors must be sensitive to all the difficulties that arise when a study is fielded.

Mr. Sheatsley is Director of the National Opinion Research Center's Survey Research Service at the University of Chicago. He has served as president of the American Association for Public Opinion Research and is the author of numerous articles on interviewing methods and practices.

5. The Harassed Respondent: II. Interviewing Practices*

PAUL B. SHEATSLEY

The term "respondent harassment" or "respondent abuse" is, of course, a loaded one. Nobody, I surmise, wants to harass respondents. Everybody would agree that they should not be abused. But what constitutes respondent abuse? How do we define it? And assuming we can define it, how prevalent is the practice? What effects, if any, does it have? What can we do about it? I address myself to the subject rather gingerly because factual information on the matter is conspicuously absent.

We all have general ideas about what constitutes respondent abuse. The editor of this book has previously referred to some of them: excessively long interviews, for example; omnibus type questionnaires which skip erratically from one unrelated subject to another; so-called depth interviews on subjects of no interest or concern to the respondent; excessive use of the telephone for survey purposes; excessive reinterviewing of panel populations; interviewer calls at unsuitable hours of the day or night, and so on.

Well, let me confess. The two-hour interview, while not exactly routine, is still not uncommon at the National Opinion Research Center. (I was engaged in one study in which the interview averaged three hours. That, I might mention, is too long.) NORC has an omnibus questionnaire service, in which we have no hesitation at all in mixing up batteries of questions about such diverse issues as the war in Viet Nam, personal drinking habits, the Negro protest movement, and attitudes toward water fluoridation or premarital sex. Gallup, Opinion Research Corporation, Alfred Politz, and a host of state and local polls regularly issue similar omnibus surveys. I confess more. NORC is presently engaged right here in New York in making callbacks, either by telephone or in person, every month for 12 months to the mothers of infants in their first year of life. This is, incidentally, after an original interview which lasted one hour and three-quarters. We are now in our tenth month of these callbacks and 89 per cent of the cases are still with us. On the last callback, only 2 per cent of them were rated by interviewers as less than cooperative. Indeed, we have

*Presented to the Market Research Council, October 15, 1965.

successfully administered a one-hour interview schedule to a widely dispersed population of doctors entirely by long-distance telephone.

I think it is clear that one cannot devise any objective definition of respondent harassment or abuse. A 30-minute interview is not necessarily a pleasant experience. A 60-minute interview is not necessarily harassment. What defines respondent abuse is the respondent's own reaction to the task imposed on him. If he feels abused by the interviewer's demands, we have to assume that he *is* abused, no matter how interesting and simple we thought our questionnaire was. If he enjoys the experience, however lengthy or complicated or uninteresting the questionnaire may seem to someone else, it is difficult to charge any abuse. The role of the interviewer, therefore, becomes an important factor in the equation. A personable and sensitive interviewer can often turn a difficult interview into an enjoyable and challenging experience for the respondent. An aggressive or uncertain interviewer can make the respondent feel uncomfortable and annoyed even though the survey itself is well designed. Two things, then, are required if the respondent is to accept his task cheerfully, without feelings of harassment and abuse. He must, first, accept the goals of the survey and feel that he is participating in something useful; and he must, second, react in a positive way to the interviewer.

In a study conducted recently for the National Health Survey by the Survey Research Center at the University of Michigan,* a team of researchers studying the factors which make for valid reporting in the interviewing situation identified—on the basis of personal observations of interviews and informal talks with respondents later—five major reasons for the feelings which respondents had about the interview. Three of these five represented areas of respondent concern. First, there was concern about the time the interview would take, that it would interfere with other activities or require an inappropriate amount of time. Second, there was concern about the questions to be asked: Will they be too personal, too demanding, repetitious, or otherwise unpleasant? Third, there was concern about the purpose or uses of the survey: Why is the information required; who will use it; for what purpose; and will the respondent have any later cause to regret his participation?

Against these three concerns, two positive factors were noted. First was an interest in the chance to be of public service or to help a worthy cause. Most people *wanted* to help. Second was an interest in the chance to interact with the interviewer. Many respondents were lonely or flattered to be asked or just plain friendly, and they were glad to converse with someone who was interested in them.

Now, if this analysis is correct, it is clear that the interviewer, as she makes her first approach to the respondent and as she begins and proceeds

*"The Influence of Interviewer and Respondent Psychological and Behavioral Variables on the Reporting in Household Interviews," National Center for Health Statistics, Series 2, No. 26, U.S. Dept. of Health, Education and Welfare, Public Health Service.

with the interview, has two things going for her: the ordinary person's interest in helping with something worthwhile and in interacting with another human being. However, there are also the three concerns of the respondent which threaten the interviewer's success: concern about the time the interview will take, about the kinds of questions to be asked, and about the purpose or use of the study. It is the interviewer's task to maintain and support the two favorable predispositions and to reassure the respondent, by both word and deed, about his three areas of concern.

I submit that respondent abuse occurs when the respondent's anxieties are *not* relieved and when the progress of the interview may even serve to reinforce them. He is concerned about the time required, but the interview goes on and on. He is concerned about the kinds of questions he will be asked, and he is confronted with one after another which strike him as silly, repetitious, overly personal, or entirely too demanding. He is concerned about the purpose and use of the survey, but he has received no straight answer, and the content of the survey seems trivial or threatening.

It is a tribute to the strength of the two favorable factors I have mentioned and to the immense goodwill of the American people that respondents so willingly put up with all that we demand of them. I suppose there are surveys in which one-third or more of the respondents at some point say to the interviewer: "Enough of this. I won't answer any more." But I don't know of any such surveys. On the contrary, I think most of us find that only 1 or 2 or 3 per cent at most ever break off an interview once they have started it. Once committed, people tend to see it through, no matter how much they may suffer.

It would be better for all if they did not, for observe what happens in such circumstances. The two essentials of a useful interview have not been met: the respondent has not been persuaded to accept the goals of the survey, and he is unable to react in a positive way to the interviewer as long as that individual is making him uncomfortable. First, then, the quality of the data suffers. The respondent becomes surly, suggests skipping certain questions, keeps repeating "I don't know," or answers unthinkingly or at random. If this happens in any considerable proportion of the cases, the effects are obvious.

Second, what does the interviewer do when faced with such a situation? Her task has become impossible. If she continues to follow her instructions in order to please her employer, her already bad rapport will continue to deteriorate, and she knows already that she is not getting good answers. On the other hand, if she wants to remotivate the respondent to accept the survey, she can do so only by skipping questions, rewording them, or otherwise disobeying instructions. Some interviewers will doggedly carry on. Some will withdraw and simply fake the missing data. Most will compromise somehow, asking enough questions to get a kind of feel for the respondent's views and then filling in the rest themselves on the basis of what they feel pretty sure the respondent would have said.

What the interviewer ought to do, of course, is to apologize to the respondent, break off the interview (or if time is the annoying factor, suggest completing it at a more convenient time), and report what happened to her supervisor. But this would be contrary to everything she has been taught. To complete the quota, to get the interview, is really "the name of the game." If she can't do it, it reflects on her. Her supervisor will tell her that all the other interviewers produced completed interviews; what's wrong with her? (Or the agency will tell the supervisor that all the other supervisors produced completed interviews; what's wrong with her staff?)

The second effect, then, of respondent abuse, besides insufficient or incorrect data, is a demoralization of the interviewer which will reflect itself either in what we call cheating behavior or in a high interviewer turnover. (I might say, incidentally, that I do not believe interviewers can be divided into good guys and bad guys or honest ones vs. cheaters. If properly selected and trained, I have found that 95 per cent of all interviewers will try their level best, sometimes beyond the call of duty, to perform as instructed. However, if asked to do what clearly turns out to be impossible, or impossibly frustrating, 95 per cent of those who don't quit will be forced into some kind of cheating or corner-cutting.)

There is, of course, yet one more effect, and that is the public relations problem about which I know some of us feel very strongly. Consider what happens when the hypothetical abused respondent we have been talking about finally gets rid of that badgering interviewer. What does he tell his family and friends about survey research? And what is likely to be his reaction, and his family's reaction, and his friends' reactions, when the next interviewer comes around with another survey?

How much respondent abuse exists? It is difficult to estimate the magnitude. We badly need a periodic sample survey of all market and survey research interviewers and we badly need continuing measurements of the public's experiences with and attitudes toward interviewers and surveys. We can all cite horrible examples, but we have no real means of assessing their impact.

My own feeling is that the problem has not yet become critical. At least, we at NORC have noticed no long-term trend toward lower completion rates or a higher proportion of refusals and breakoffs. I must admit, of course, that a small proportion of our respondents on any given survey do not enjoy the interview and that a particular question item or procedure is sometimes criticized by many interviewers. But by and large our respondents do not seem to feel abused, judging from their repeated cooperation on panel studies, the time and effort they have been willing to give us, and their own statements as to how interesting or enjoyable the interview was. But I know and you know, of course, that there is an awful lot of shoddy work in this field being done by the other guy.

Eighteen years ago I published an article in the *Public Opinion Quarterly* called "Some Uses of Interviewer Report Forms." Interviewers are asked on such forms, at the conclusion of each assignment, for their general reactions to the survey, its comparative ease or difficulty, particular questions or series of questions which respondents enjoyed, or which were found to be difficult, frequently misunderstood, embarrassing, or poorly worded. I pointed out in the article that such data from interviewers had important uses in three major respects: first, in the supervision and maintenance of the field staff by providing a regular means whereby interviewers can communicate with their supervisors; second, in the analysis and evaluation of the survey findings through the warning they provide of likely misunderstandings, biases, or inaccuracies in the data; and third, in the design and wording of future questionnaires through the advice they provide about what works and what does not.

I would plead that we all solicit the reactions and experience of our interviewers and that we pay heed to what they tell us. We can do this in pretest through meeting with the pretesters, going through the questionnaire item by item, and asking them just what problems occurred. We can do this by means of written reports after each survey, so that we can be alerted to possible kinds of respondent abuse which might not otherwise come to our attention.

It is, of course, true that our main objective is not merely to provide the interviewer and the respondent with a pleasant experience. We have research problems to solve and data that we urgently require. Sometimes the problem *demands* a two-hour interview; sometimes we simply *must* devise questions about personal or threatening subjects; sometimes it is crucial that we lead the respondent through what may seem to him repetitious questioning.

However, there *are* ways—some simple and some necessarily very ingenious—by which a competent researcher can usually manage to do these things. Essentially, they involve meeting the respondent's three major concerns about time, about the questions he's asked, and about the purpose of the questions. Often, it is simply a matter of leveling with him. If it is a one-hour interview and he was assured it would only take 20 minutes or so, he will darn well feel abused. If he wants to know what good the survey will do and your interviewer has not been provided with an acceptable answer, he is likely to feel harassed as the questioning goes on.

Besides leveling with the respondent, let's level with our interviewers. Let's abandon the myth that a good interviewer can make a respondent sit through anything without feeling harassed. If interviewers could be depended upon to tell us frankly when something doesn't work, we, and our data, and our interviewers, and our respondents would all be better off.

Let us remember that abuse is defined by the respondent. If we can get him to accept the goals of our survey and provide him with a reasonably good interviewer, he can be asked to do all sorts of things, and he will not feel abused. If he cannot be persuaded to accept our goals, the fault lies with us, and we had better do something about it.

As marketing management increases its reliance on consumer surveys, research becomes more and more a big business. As such, it begins to take on the characteristics of a mass production operation, including division of labor and specialization of responsibilities and skills. Management becomes increasingly impersonal and defines its interests as being different from those of "labor." The people who plan and direct studies are increasingly estranged in their values and goals from those who execute them.

The consequences of this alienation are described and commented upon in the next essay by Julius Roth which deals with cheating as but one of the motivational problems of the people who conduct research without a stake in its outcome or in its correctness. Professor Roth is a sociologist at the University of California at Davis. He has carried out several field studies, mostly in the area of medical care services. For the past several years, he has taught courses in sociological methods in which he emphasizes viewing research as a social process which requires the examination of the behavior of the researchers as well as the subjects.

6. Hired Hand Research*

JULIUS A. ROTH

CASE I

After it became obvious how tedious it was to write down numbers on pieces of paper which didn't even fulfill one's own sense of reality and which did not remind one of the goals of the project, we all in little ways started avoiding our work and cheating on the project. It began for example when we were supposed to be observing for hour and a half periods, an hour and a half on the ward and then an hour and a half afterwards to write up or dictate what we had observed, in terms of the category system which the project was supposed to be testing and in terms of a ward diary. We began cutting corners in time. We would arrive a little bit late and leave a little bit early. It began innocently enough, but soon boomeranged into a full cheating syndrome, where we would fake observations for some time slot which were never observed on the ward. Sam, for example, in one case, came onto the ward while I was still finishing up an assignment on a study patient and told me that he was supposed to observe for an hour and a half but that he wasn't going to stay because he couldn't stand it anymore. He said he wasn't going to tell anyone that he missed an assignment, but that he would simply write up a report on the basis of what he knew already about the ward and the patients. I was somewhat appalled by Sam's chicanery, and in this sense I was the last one to go. It was three or four weeks after this before I actually cheated in the same manner.

It was also frequent for us to miss observation periods, especially the 8 to 9:30 a.m. ones. We all had a long drive for one thing, and we were all chronic over-sleepers for another. For a while we used to make up the times we missed by coming in the next morning at the same time and submitting our reports with the previous day's date. As time went on, however, we didn't bother to make up the times we'd missed. When we were questioned by our supervisor about the missing reports, we would claim that there had been an error in scheduling and that we did not know that those time slots were supposed to be covered.

---

*Reprinted from *The American Sociologist* (August, 1966), pp. 190–196. This paper was initially prepared for the Columbia University Seminar on Content and Method in The Social Sciences, December 14, 1965.

There were other ways we would cheat, sometimes inadvertently. For example, one can decide that one can't hear enough of a conversation to record it. People need to think fairly highly of themselves, and when you think that you're a cheat and a liar and that you're not doing your job for which you are receiving high wages, you are likely to find little subconscious ways of getting out of having to accuse yourself of these things. One of the ways is to not be able to hear well. We had a special category in our coding system, a question mark, which we noted by its symbol on our code sheets whenever we could not hear what was going on between two patients. As the purgatory of writing numbers on pieces of paper lengthened, more and more transcripts were passed in with question marks on them, so that even though we had probably actually heard most of the conversations between patients, we were still actually avoiding the work of transcription by deceiving ourselves into believing that we could not hear what was being said. This became a good way of saving yourself work. If you couldn't hear a conversation, it just got one mark in one column of one code sheet, and if you wrote down an elaborate conversation lasting even ten minutes, it might take you up to an hour to code it, one hour of putting numbers in little blocks. In the long run, all of our data became much skimpier. Conversations were incomplete; their duration was strangely diminishing to two or three minutes in length instead of the half-hour talks the patients usually had with each other. We were all defining our own cutting off points, saying to ourselves, "Well, that's enough of that conversation." According to the coding rules, however, a communication can't be considered as ended until the sequence of interaction has been completed and a certain time lapse of silence has ensued.

In order to ensure the reliability of our coding, the research design called for an "Inter-Rater Reliability Check" once every two months, in which each of the four of us would pair up with every other member of the team and be rated on our ability to code jointly the same interaction in terms of the same categories and dimensions. We learned to loathe these checks; we knew that the coding system was inadequate in terms of reliability and that our choice of categories was optional, subjective, and largely according to our own sense of what an interaction is really about, rather than according to the rigid, stylized, and preconceived design into which we were supposed to make reality fit. We also knew, however, that our principal investigators insisted on an inter-rater reliability coefficient of .70 in order for the research to proceed. When the time came for another check, we met together to discuss and make certain agreements on how to bring our coding habits into conformity for the sake of achieving reliability. In these meetings we would confess our preferences for coding certain things in certain ways and agree on certain concessions to each other for the duration of the check. Depending on what other individual I was to be paired with, for example, I had a very good idea of how I could code in order to achieve nearly the same transcriptions. We didn't end it there. After each phase of a check, each pair of us would meet again to go over our transcriptions and compare our coding, and if there were any gross discrepancies, we corrected them before sending them to the statistician for analysis. Needless to say, as soon as the reliability checks were over with, we each returned to a coding rationale which we as individuals required in order to do any coding at all—in order to maintain sanity.

CASE II

There didn't appear to be too much concern with the possibility of inconsistency among the coders. Various coders used various methods to determine the code of an open-end question. Toward the end of the coding process, expediency became the keynote, leading to gross inconsistency. The most expedient method of coding a few of the trickier questions was to simply put down a "4" (this was the middle-of-the-road response on the one question that had the most variation). If the responses were not clear or comprehensible, the coder had two alternatives: on the one hand, he could puzzle over it and ask for other opinions or, on the other hand, he could assign it an arbitrary number or forget the response entirely.

In the beginning, many of us, when in doubt about a response, would ask the supervisor or his assistant. After a while, I noted that quite often the supervisor's opinion would differ when asked twice about the same response and he would often give two different answers in response to the same question. One way the supervisor and his assistant would determine the correct coding for an answer would be to look at the respondent's previous answers and deduce what they should have answered—thereby coding on *what they thought the respondent should have answered*, not on the basis of what he *did* answer. One example that I distinctly remember is the use of magazines regularly read as reported by the respondent being used as a basis on which to judge and code their political views. This, in my opinion, would be a factor in some of the cases, such as the reading of an extreme leftist or extreme rightist magazine, but to use magazines such as *Time* or *Reader's Digest* to form any conclusions about the type of person and his views, I feel is quite arbitrary. Furthermore, I feel questionnaires should be used to see if consistent patterns of views exist among respondents and it is not the coder's job to put them in if the respondents fail to!

Some of the coders expected a fixed pattern of response. I, not being sure of what responses meant in a total political profile, treated each response separately—which I feel is the correct way of coding a questionnaire. Others, as I learned through their incessant jabbering, took what they thought was a more sophisticated method of treating an interview. A few would discuss the respondent's answers as if they took one political or social standpoint as an indicator of what all the responses should be. They would laugh over an inconsistency in the respondent's replies, feeling that one answer did not fit the previous pattern of responses.

The final problem leading to gross inconsistency was the factor of time.

The supervisor made it clear that the code sheets had to be in to the computation center by Saturday. This meant that on Saturday morning and early afternoon the aim of the coders was to code the questionnaires as quickly as possible, and the crucial factor was speed, even at the expense of accuracy. The underlying thought was that there were so many questionnaires coded already (that were *assumed* to be coded consistently and correctly) that the inconsistencies in the remainder would balance themselves out and be of no great importance. I found myself adapting to this way of thinking, and after spending two or three hours there on Saturday morning, I joined in the game of "let's get these damn things out already." It did indeed become a game, with the shibboleth, for one particularly vague and troublesome question, "Oh, give it a four."

CASE III

One of the questions on the interview schedule asked for five reasons why parents had put their child in an institution. I found most people can't think of five reasons. One or two—sometimes three. At first I tried pumping them for more reasons, but I never got any of them up to five. I didn't want (the director) to think I was goofing off on the probing, so I always filled in all five.

Another tough one was the item about how the child's disability affected the family relationships. We were supposed to probe. Probe what? You get so many different kinds of answers, I was never sure what was worth following up. Sometimes I did if the respondent seemed to have something to say. Otherwise I just put down a short answer and made it look as if that was all I could get out of them. Of course, (the director) *did* list a few areas he wanted covered in the probing. One of them was sex relations of the parents. Most of the time I didn't follow up on that. Once in a while I would get somebody who seemed to be able to talk freely without embarrassment. But most of the time I was afraid to ask, so I made up something to fill that space.

Then there was that wide open question at the end. It's vague. Most people don't know what to say. You've been asking them questions for about an hour already. Usually you get a very short answer. I didn't push them. I'd write up a longer answer later. It's easy to do. You have their answers to a lot of other questions to draw on. You just put parts of some of them together, dress it up a little, and add one or two bits of new information which fits in with the rest.

Any reader with research experience can probably recall one or more cases in which he observed, suspected, or participated in some form of cheating, carelessness, distortion, or cutting of corners in the collection or processing of research data. He probably thought of these instances as exceptions—an unfortunate lapse in ethical behavior or a failure of research directors to maintain proper controls. I would like to put forth the thesis that such behavior on the part of hired data-collectors and processors is not abnormal or exceptional, but rather is exactly the kind of behavior we should expect from people with their position in a production unit.

The cases I have presented do not constitute proof, of course. Even if I presented ten or twenty more, my efforts could be dismissed as merely an unusually industrious effort to record professional dirty linen (or I might be accused of making them up!) and not at all representative of the many thousands of cases of hired researching carried out every year. Rather than multiply examples, I would like to take a different tack and examine the model we have been using in thinking about research operations and to suggest another model which I believe is more appropriate.

The ideal we hold of the researcher is that of a well-educated scholar pursuing information and ideas on problems in which he has an intrinsic interest. Frequently this ideal may be approximated when an individual scholar is working on his own problem or several colleagues are collaborating on a problem of mutual interest. Presumably such a researcher will endeavor to carry out his data-collection and processing in the most accurate and useful way that his skills and time permit.

When a researcher hires others to do the collecting and processing tasks of his research plan, we often assume that these assistants fit the "dedicated scientist" ideal and will lend their efforts to the successful conduct of the over-all study by carrying out their assigned tasks to the best of their ability. As suggested by my examples, I doubt that hired assistants usually behave this way even when they are junior grade scholars themselves. It becomes more doubtful yet when they are even further removed from scholarly tradition and from the direct control of the research directors (e.g., part-time survey interviewers).

It seems to me that we can develop a more accurate expectation of the contribution of the hired research worker who is required to work according to somebody else's plan by applying another model which has been worked out in some detail by sociologists—namely, the work behavior of the hired hand in a production organization. First, let us look at one of the more thorough of these studies, Donald Roy's report on machine shop operators.[1]

Roy's workers made the job easier by loafing when the piece rate did not pay well. They were careful not to go over their informal "quotas" on piece rate jobs because the rate would be cut and their work would be harder. They faked time sheets so that their actual productive abilities would not be known to management. They cut corners on prescribed job procedures to make the work easier and/or more lucrative even though this sometimes meant that numerous products had to be scrapped. Roy's calculations show that the workers could have produced on the order of twice as much if it had been in their interest to do so.

But it is *not* in their interest to do so. The product the hired hand

[1] Donald Roy, "Quota Restriction and Goldbricking in a Machine Shop," *American Journal of Sociology,* 57 (March, 1952), pp. 427–442.

turns out is not in any sense his. He does not design it, make any of the decisions about producing it or about the conditions under which it will be produced, or what will be done with it after it is produced. The worker is interested in doing just enough to get by. Why should he concern himself about how well the product works or how much time it takes to make it? That is the company's problem. The company is his adversary and fair game for any trickery he can get away with. The worker's aim is to make his job as easy and congenial as the limited resources allow and to make as much money as possible without posing a threat to his fellow workers or to his own future. The company, in turn, is placed in the position of having to establish an inspection system to try to keep the worst of their products from leaving the factory (an effort often unsuccessful—the inspectors are hired hands, too) and of devising some form of supervision to limit the more extreme forms of gold-bricking and careless workmanship.

Almost all the systematic research on "restriction of output" and deviation from assigned duties has been done on factory workers, office clerks, and other low prestige work groups. This is mostly because such work is easier to observe and measure, but also because much of this research has been controlled in part by those in a position of authority who want research done only on their subordinates. However, there is evidence to indicate that work restrictions and deviations in the form of informal group definitions and expectations are probably universal in our society. They can be found among business executives and in the professions, sports, and the creative arts. They are especially likely to crop up when one is working as a hired hand, and almost all productive activities have their hired hand aspects. A professor may work hard on scholarly tasks of his own choosing and perhaps even on teaching a course which he himself has devised, but he becomes notoriously lax when he is assigned to a departmental service course which he does not like—spending little or no time on preparation, avoiding his students as much as possible, turning all the exams over to a graduate assistant, and so on.

"Restriction of production" and deviation from work instructions is no longer regarded by students of the sociology of work as a moral issue or a form of social delinquency. Rather, it is the expected behavior of workers in a production organization. The only problem for an investigator of work practices is discovering the details of cutting corners, falsifying time sheets, defining work quotas, dodging supervision, and ignoring instructions in a given work setting.

There is no reason to believe that a hired hand in the scientific research business will behave any differently from those in other areas of productive activity. It is far more reasonable to assume that their behavior will be similar. They want to make as much money as they can and may pad their account or time sheet if they are paid on that basis, but this type of behavior is a minor problem so far as the present discussion is concerned. They also want to avoid difficult, embarrassing, inconvenient, time-consuming situations as well as those activities which make no sense to them. (Thus, they fail to make some assigned observations or to ask some of the interview questions.) At the same time they want to give the right impression to their superiors—at least right enough so that their material will be accepted and they will be kept on the job. (Thus, they modify or fabricate portions of the reports in order to give the boss what he *seems* to want.) They do not want to "look stupid" by asking too many questions, so they are likely to make a stab at what they think the boss wants—e.g., make a guess at a coding category rather than having it resolved through channels.

Even those who start out with the notion that this is an important piece of work which they must do right will succumb to the hired-hand mentality when they realize that their suggestions and criticisms are ignored, that their assignment does not allow for any imagination or creativity, that they will receive no credit for the final product, in short, that they have been hired to do somebody else's dirty work. When this realization has sunk in, they will no longer bother to be careful or accurate or precise. They will cut corners to save time and energy. They will fake parts of their reporting. They will not put themselves out for something in which they have no stake except in so far as extrinsic pressures force them to. Case No. I is an excerpt from the statement of a research worker who started out with enthusiasm and hard work and ended with sloppy work and cheating when she could no longer escape the fact that she was a mere flunky expected to do her duty whether or not it was meaningful. The coders in Case II soon gave up any effort to resolve the ambiguities of their coding operation and followed the easiest path acceptable to their supervisor. In this case, the supervisor himself made little effort to direct the data-processing toward supplying answers to meaningful research issues. We must remember that in many research operations the supervisors and directors themselves are hired hands carrying out the requests of a client or superior as expeditiously as possible.

Many of the actions of hired hand researchers are strikingly analogous to restrictive practices of factory operatives. Interviewers who limit probing and observers who limit interaction recording are behaving like workers applying "quota restriction," and with interacting hired hands informal agreements may be reached on the extent of such restrictions. To fabricate portions of a report is a form of goldbricking. The collusion on the reliability check reported in Case I is strikingly similar to the workers' plot to mislead the time-study department. Such similarities are no accident. The relationship of the hired hand to the product and the process of production is the same in each case. The product is not "his." The production process gives him little or no opportunity to express any intrinsic interest he may have in the product. He will sooner or later fall into a pattern of carrying out his work with a minimum of effort, inconvenience, and embarrassment—doing just enough so that his product will get by. If he is part of a large and complex operation where his immediate superiors are also hired hands with no intrinsic interest in the product and where the final authority may be distant and even amorphous, quality control of the product will be mechanical and the minimal effort that will get by can soon be learned and easily applied. The factory production situation has at least one ultimate limitation on the more extreme deviations of the hired hands: the final product must "work" reasonably well in a substantial proportion of cases. In social science research, on the other hand, the product is usually so ambiguous and the field of study so lacking in standards of performance, that it is difficult for anyone to say whether it "works" or not.

What is more important is the effect of the hired hand mentality on the *nature* of the product. Workmen not only turn out less than they could if it were in their interest to maximize production, but often produce shoddy and even dangerous products.[2] In the case of research, the inefficiency of hired hands not only causes a study to take longer or cost more money, but is likely to introduce much dubious data and interpretations into the process of analysis. Our mass production industrial system has opted to sacrifice individual efficiency and product quality for the advantages of a rationalized division of labor. The same approach has been applied to much of our larger scale scientific research and the results, in my opinion, have been much more disastrous than they are in industrial production with little of the compensating advantages.

When the tasks of a research project are split up into small pieces to be assigned to hired hands, none of these data-collectors and processors will ever understand all the complexities and subtleties of the research issues in the same way as the person who conceived of the study. No amount of "training" can take the place of the gradual development of research interests and formulations on the part of the planner. Since the director often cannot be sure what conceptions of the issues the hired hands have as a result of his explanations and "training," he must make dubious guesses about the meaning of much of the data they return to him. If he attempts to deal with this difficulty by narrowly defining the permissible behavior of each hired hand (e.g., demand that all questions on a schedule be asked in a set wording), he merely increases the alienation of the hired hand from his work and thus increases the likelihood of cutting corners and cheating. As he gains in quantity of data, he loses in validity and meaningfulness.[3]

I do not want to give the impression that the hired hand mentality with its attendant difficulties is simply a characteristic of the large-scale ongoing research organization. We may find it at all size levels, including the academic man hiring a single student to do his research chores. The argument may be advanced that assignment of specified tasks by the director of

[2] I want to emphasize once again that in a business setting, supervisors and executives, as well as production line workmen, participate in aspects of the hired hand mentality. None of them may have an intrinsic interest in the quality of the product. (See, for example, Melville Dalton, *Men Who Manage*, New York: John Wiley and Sons, Inc., 1959, especially Chapters 7,8, and 9.) The same is the case in much large-scale research.

[3] In this discussion I am assuming there *is* some one (or a small group of colleagues) who has initially formulated the research problem or area of concern because of intrinsic interest and curiosity. In much of our social science research, we do not have even this saving grace and the research is formulated and carried out for various "political" reasons. In such cases, we cannot count on having anyone interested enough to try to turn the accumulations of data into a meaningful explanatory statement.

a study is essential to getting the job done in the manner that he wants it done. My answer is that such assignments are often not effectively carried out and it is misleading to assume that they are.

Let me illustrate this point. A researcher wants to do a study of the operation of a given institution. He has some definite notion of what aspects of behavior of the institutional personnel he wants information about and he has some ideas about the manner in which he will go about analysing and interpreting these behaviors. He finds it possible and useful to engage four trained and interested assistants. Let me outline two ways the study might be conducted:

A. Through a series of discussions, general agreement is reached about the nature of the study and the manner in which it might be conducted. Some division of labor is agreed upon in these discussions. However, none of the field workers is held to any particular tasks or foci of interest. Each is allowed to pursue his data-collection as he thinks best within the larger framework, although the field workers exchange information frequently and make new agreements so that they can benefit from each other's experience.

B. The director divides up the data-collection and processing in a logical manner and assigns a portion to each of the assistants. Each field worker is instructed to obtain information in all the areas assigned to him and to work in a prescribed manner so that his information will be directly comparable to that of the others. The director may use a procedural check such as having each assistant write a report covering given issues or areas at regular intervals.

Which is the preferred approach? Judging from my reading of social science journals, most research directors would say Method B is to be preferred. Method A, they would maintain, produces information on subjects, issues, or events from one field worker which is not directly comparable to that collected by another field worker. They would also object that if each field worker is permitted to follow his own inclinations even in part, the total study will suffer from large gaps. These accusations are quite true—and, I would add, are an inevitable result of dividing a research project among a number of people. What I disagree with, however, is the assumption that Method B would not suffer from these defects (if indeed, they should be regarded as defects). It is assumed that the assistants in Method B are actually carrying out their assigned tasks in the manner specified. In line with my earlier discussion of the behavior of hired hands, I would consider this highly unlikely. If the information produced by these assistants is indeed closely comparable, it would most likely be because they had reached an agreement on how to restrict production. And, whether the study is carried out by Method A or by Method B, gaps will occur. The difference is that the director of Study A—assuming he had succeeded in making his assistants into collaborating colleagues—would at least know where the gaps are. The director of Study B would have gaps without knowing where they are—or indeed, that they exist—because they have been covered over by the fabrications of his alienated assistants.

It is ironic that established researchers do not ascribe the same motivating forces to their subordinates as they do to themselves. For many years research scientists have been confronting those who pay their salaries and give them their grants with the argument that a scientist can do good research only when he has the freedom to follow his ideas in whatever way seems best. They have been so successful with this argument that university administrations and research organization directorates rarely attempt to dictate—or even suggest—problems or procedures to a researcher on their staff, and the more prominent granting agencies write contracts with almost no strings attached as to the way in which the study will be conducted. Yet research directors fail to apply this same principle to those they hire to carry out data-collection and processing. The hired assistant's desire to participate in the task and the creative contribution he might make is ignored with the result that the assistants' creativity is applied instead to covertly changing the nature of the task.

There has been very little discussion in our journals and our books on research methods on the relationship of the hired hand to the data collected. Whatever discussion there *has* been can be found in the survey interview field where there have been some studies of the effect of such demographic factors as age, sex, and race, sometimes measured personality traits, on "interviewer bias." The nature of the interviewer's status in a research organization is seldom discussed in print. The problem of interviewer cheating, although a common subject of informal gossip, is seldom dealt with openly as a serious problem. When Leo Crespi published an article twenty years ago in which he expressed the worry that cheating was seriously affecting the validity of much survey data,[4] those who responded (mostly survey organization executives) stated reassuringly that few interviewers cheated and that they had pretty effective ways of controlling those who did.[5] If the analysis offered in this paper is correct, the first part of this reassurance is almost certainly wrong. The low level flunky position which most interviewers occupy in survey organizations[6] should lead us to expect widespread deviations from assigned tasks. The survey executives who responded give no convincing evidence to the contrary. As for the second part of the assertion, their descriptions of their control measures indicate that they can hope to block only the cruder, more obvious, and repeated forms of cheating. The postal card follow-up will catch the interviewer who does not bother to contact his respondents at all. Spot-check follow-up interviewing may eventually catch the interviewer who makes contacts, but fabricates demographic data (to fill a quota sample) or completes only

[4] Leo Crespi, "The Cheater Problem in Polling," *Public Opinion Quarterly*, Winter 1945–1946, pp. 431–445.

[5] "Survey on Problems of Interviewer Cheating," *International Journal of Opinion and Attitude Research*, 1 (1947), pp. 93–107.

[6] Julius A. Roth, "The Status of Interviewing," *The Midwest Sociologist*, 19 (December, 1956), pp. 8–11.

part of the interview and fills in the rest in a stereotyped manner later on. (Even here, many of his interviews may be used before he is detected.) However, from the cases of hired hand interviewing which I am familiar with, I would say such crude cheating is not the most common form of cutting corners on the job. Far more common is the kind found in Case III where the interviewer makes his contact, obtains a fairly complete interview, but leaves partial gaps here and there because he found it time-consuming, embarrassing, or troublesome, felt threatened by the respondent, or simply felt uncertain about how the study director wanted certain lines of questioning developed. With a little imagination, such gaps can be filled in later on in a way that is very unlikely to be detected in a follow-up interview. If, for example, a supervisor in Case III had returned to the respondents and asked them whether the "five reasons" listed on their interview form were accurate reflections of their opinion, probably most would have said yes, and the few who objected to one or two of the reasons could have been dismissed as the degree of change that one expects on re-interview.[7]

Some gimmicks for catching cheaters may even put the finger on the wrong person. Thus, one approach to detecting cheating is to compare the data of each interviewer to the group averages and to assume that if one deviates markedly from the group, he is cheating or doing his work improperly. This reasoning assumes that cheating is exceptional and will stand out from the crowd. I have already suggested that the opposite is often the case. Therefore, if the cheaters are working in the same direction (which is readily possible if they have reached an informal agreement or if the question is of such a nature as to suggest distortion in a given direction), it is the "honest" person who will deviate. In the study alluded to in Case III, for example, one of the interviewers always left spaces open on the "five reasons" item. At one point the director reprimanded him for not obtaining five responses "like the rest of the interviewers." The director preferred to believe that this man was not doing his job right than to believe that all the rest were making up responses.

Large survey organizations have at least made some attempts to control the cruder forms of cheating. In most studies using hired hands, even this limited control is absent. The academic man with one or a few assistants, the research organization study director with one or a few small projects, usually has no routine way of checking on the work of his assistants. If he duplicates much of their work or supervises them very closely, he may as well dispense with their services. If he gives them assignments without checking on them closely, he is in effect assuming that they are conducting their assignment more or less as directed and is accepting their products at face value. This assumption, I assert, is a dubious one. And since it is a

[7] I have even heard the argument that it makes no difference if perceptive interviewers make up parts of the interview responses with the help of information from other responses because their fabrications will usually closely approximate what the subject would have said if he could have been prompted to answer. But if we accept this argument, a large portion of the interview should have been eliminated to begin with. It means we already claim to know the nature of some of the relationships which the study is purportedly investigating.

common practice nowadays to farm out much of one's research work—quite often to accumulate research grants only to hire others to do the bulk of the work—the dubious nature of hired hand research is a widespread problem in small- as well as large-scale research, in surveys, in direct observation, and in various forms of data processing.

I do not want to suggest, however, that the major failure of hired hand research is the lack of control of cheating. Rather, the very fact that we are placed in a position of having to think up gimmicks to detect cheating is in itself an admission of failure. It means that we are relying for an important part of our research operation on people who have no concern for the outcome of the study. Such persons cannot have the kind of understanding of the data-collection or data-processing procedures which can come only with working out problems in which the researcher has an intrinsic interest and has gone through a process of formulating research questions and relevant ways of collecting and processing data.

I can hear the objection that much social science cannot be done without hired hands. But we should at least be aware of the doubtful nature of some of the information collected in this way and construct our data-collection and processing in such a way as to reduce the encouragement of cheating and restriction of production as much as possible. (See Crespi's list of "ballot demoralizers."[8]) More important, however, I believe the need for hired hands has been greatly exaggerated. Why, for example, must we so often have large samples? The large sample is frequently a contrivance for controlling various kinds of "errors" (including the "error" introduced by unreliable hired hands). But if the study were done on a much smaller sample by one person or several colleagues who formulated their own study and conducted it entirely by themselves, much of this error would not enter in the first place. Isn't a sample of fifty which yields data in which we can have a high degree of confidence more useful than a sample of five thousand where we must remain doubtful about what it is that we have collected? Often a large-scale study tries to do too much at one time and so ends up as a hodge-podge affair with no integration of ideas or information ever taking place because it is, in effect, *nobody's* study. How often have you read the report of a massive study expending large amounts of money and employing large numbers of people where you were disappointed at the paucity of the results, especially when compared to a far smaller project on a similar issue conducted entirely by one or a few people?

Let me repeat that I am not singling out large-scale operations as the only villains. The current structure of professional careers is such that often small studies are turned over to hired hands. We tend to be rated on how many studies we can carry on at the same time rather than on how thoroughly and carefully we can carry through a given line of research. Soon

[8] Leo Crespi, *op. cit.*, pp. 437–439.

we find that we do not have time for all of the projects we have become involved in and must turn some over to others of lower professional status. This might not be so bad if we were willing to turn over the research work wholeheartedly. We might simply act as entrepreneurs to funnel funds to others and to provide them with appropriate clearance and an entré to research settings. We can then leave the specific formulation of the problem and procedure (and the credit for doing the work) to the person we have helped out. Such is often done, of course. However, there are many instances in which the senior researcher believes those he has hired cannot be trusted to formulate their own plans, or professional career competition convinces him that he cannot "afford" to give up any of his studies to others. In such cases he is likely to maintain a semblance of control by mechanically structuring a research plan and making assignments to his assistants. This, as I have indicated, is the way to the hired hand mentality with its attendant distortions of research data.

What is a hired hand? So far I have been talking as if I knew and as if the hired hand could readily be distinguished from one who is not. This, of course, is not true. The issue is a complex one and information on it is, by its very nature, not very accessible. It is a crucial question which deserves study in its own right as part of the more general study of the process of "doing research."

Let me attempt a crude characterization of hired hand research, a characterization which hopefully will be greatly refined and perhaps reformulated with further study. A hired hand is a person who feels that he has no stake in the research that he is working on, that he is simply expected to carry out assigned tasks and turn in results which will "pass inspection." Of course, a hired assistant may not start out with the hired hand mentality, but may develop it if he finds that his talents for creativity are not called upon and that his suggestions and efforts at active participation are ignored.

From specific examples from the research world and by analogy from research on hired hands in other occupational spheres, I am convinced that research tasks carried out by hired hands are characterized, not rarely or occasionally, but *typically*, by restricted production, failure to carry out portions of the task, avoidance of the more unpleasant or difficult aspects of the research, and outright cheating. The results of research done in part or wholly by hired hands should be viewed as a dubious source for information about specific aspects of our social life or for the raw material for developing broader generalizations.

Of course, this leaves open the question of what constitutes a "stake in the research" and how one avoids or reduces the hired hand mentality. Again, I have no specific answers and hope that issue will receive much more attention than it has up to now. A stake may mean different things in various circumstances. For graduate students, a chance to share in planning and in writing and publication may often be important. For interviewers or field workers, the determination of the details of their procedure may be crucial. In an applied setting, the responsibility for the practical consequences of the research findings may be most important.[9]

It would also be worthwhile to examine the conditions which make for hired hand research. Here again, I have little specific to say and this subject, too, needs much more investigation. However, I will suggest a few factors I consider important.

Size. Hired hands can be found in research staffs of all sizes from one on up. However, it is clear that when a very small number of researchers are working together, there is a greater possibility of developing a true colleagueship in which each will be able to formulate some of his own ideas and put them into action. The larger the group, the more difficult this becomes until the point is probably reached where it is virtually impossible, and the organization must be run on the basis of hierarchical staff relations with the lower echelons almost inevitably becoming hired hands.

Subordination. If some members of the research group are distinctly subordinate to others in a given organizational hierarchy or in general social status, it will be more difficult to develop a true colleague working relationship than if their status were more closely equal. The subordinate may hesitate to advance his ideas; the superordinate might be loath to admit that his lower-level co-worker be entitled to inject his ideas into the plans. Formal super-subordinate relationships can of course be muted and sometimes completely overcome in the course of personal contact, but certainly this is an initial, and sometimes permanent, basis for establishing hired hand status.

Adherence to Rigid Plans. If a researcher believes that good research can be done only if a detailed plan of data-collection, processing, and analysis is established in advance and adhered to throughout, he has laid the basis for hired hand research if he makes use of assistance from others who have not participated in the original plan. Sticking to a pre-formed plan means that others cannot openly introduce variations which may make the study more meaningful for them. Any creativity they apply will be of a surreptitious nature.

In their research methods texts, our students are told a great deal about the mechanics of research technique and little about the social process of researching. What little is said on the latter score consists largely of Pollyannaish statements about morale, honesty, and "proper motivation." It should be noted that appeals to morality and patriotism never reduced goldbricking and restriction of production in industry, even during the time of a world war. There is no reason to believe that analogous appeals to interviewers, graduate students, research assistants, and others who serve as hired hands will be any more effective. If we want to avoid the hired hand mentality, we must stop using people as hired hands.

Glaser and Strauss state that we regularly "discount" aspects of many,

[9] The "human relations in industry" movement has given us some useful suggestions about the circumstances which alienate workers and executives, and also ways in which industrial employees may be given a real stake in their jobs. See, for example, Douglas McGregor, *The Human Side of Enterprise*, New York: McGraw-Hill Book Co., 1960, Part 2.

if not most, of all scientific analyses we read because we consider the research design one-sided, believe that it does not fit the social structure to which it was generalized, or that it does not fit in with our observations in an area where we have had considerable experience.[10]

I would like to suggest another area in which we might consistently apply the "discounting process." When reading a research report, we should pay close attention to the description of how the data was collected, processed, analyzed, interpreted, and written up with an eye to determining what part, if any, was played by hired hands. This will often be a difficult and highly tentative judgement, requiring much reading between the lines with the help of our knowledge of how our colleagues and we ourselves often operate. However, we can get hints from such things as the size of the staff, the nature of the relationship of the staff members, the manner in which the research plans were developed and applied, the organizational setting in which the research was done, mention made of assignment of tasks, and so on. If there is good reason to believe that significant parts of the research have been carried out by hired hands, this would, in my opinion, be a reason for discounting much or all of the results of the study.

---

[10] Barney Glaser and Anselm L. Strauss, "Discovery of Substantive Theory: A Basic Strategy Underlying Qualitative Research," *American Behavioral Scientist,* 8 (February, 1965), pp. 5–12.

The problem of motivating the fieldworker and of checking on the accuracy of his performance is further pursued in the next paper. The author believes that validation procedures, originally instituted to increase the quality of field performance by establishing an independent check on interviewer performance, actually often work against the best interests of the research profession by antagonizing both the public and the interviewers on whom the accuracy of survey data depends, in the final analysis. Manfield is not merely concerned with the special problems of validation procedures. He is concerned with the entire structure of field apparatus, including the interviewers, those who supervise them, and the directors of fieldwork at the central offices of research organizations. Too often, he insists, the problems that arise in the field reflect sloppy controls at headquarters or unreasonable demands on the part of the client.

The author has been a practicing survey researcher since 1936. He has taught at the New School for Social Research, is the author of a number of articles on data collection, and is President of M.N. Manfield Associates, Inc., a research firm.

7. The Status of Validation in Survey Research

MANUEL N. MANFIELD

BACKGROUND INFORMATION RELATING TO VALIDATION

Validation is the term generally applied to those practices in research methodology designed to determine *whether* and *how* interviews were conducted. The activities to which the term applies have also been referred to as "verification" and "checking." The term "validation" is not to be confused with the like-sounding term "validity." Whereas validity pertains to the performance of the survey instruments—whether they are capable of obtaining the information for which they are designed—validation pertains to the performance of the interviewers. The former requires determination before the data for the survey are collected, and the latter requires determination after the data have been collected.

Validation, as a part of research methodology, traces back to the infancy of research. A volume entitled *The Technique of Marketing Research*[1] which was five years in preparation and was published in 1937, lists "inspectors" among the personnel needed for the data-collecting phase of research. The book states that the inspector has two basic functions: "to confirm the fact that the reported interviews actually took place and that the information obtained was correctly recorded."[2] In 1948, a committee of the American Marketing Association mentioned validation as part of fundamental marketing research techniques: "the fact that a respondent has been interviewed is a very worthwhile and necessary thing to know and constitutes the first check on the integrity of the interviewer."[3] Although validation, when mentioned in the literature, is spoken of as having a dual purpose—*whether* the interview was conducted and *how* the interview was conducted—validation, as practiced through the years, has centered on whether the interview was conducted.

---

[1] Committee on Marketing Research Techniques, American Marketing Association, *The Technique of Marketing Research* (New York: McGraw-Hill, 1937).

[2] *Ibid.*, p. 181.

[3] Committee on Marketing Research Techniques, American Marketing Association, "Selection, Training and Supervision of Field Interviewers in Marketing Research," *The Journal of Marketing* (January, 1948), p. 376.

Although validation of interviews dates back to the infancy of survey research, references relating to it in the literature are brief and incidental to other subjects. In the approximately forty years during which survey research has been practiced, validations have been conducted primarily by mail, i.e., by postcard. This, in the early years of research, was doubtlessly necessitated by the high cost of personal validations and by the relatively low proportion of homes with telephones. With the emergence of the independent local supervisor as an important factor in data collection after the Korean War, coupled with a marked increase in the proportion of homes with telephones, validation by telephone increased. The percentage of homes having telephones in the United States increased from 37 per cent in 1940 to 62 per cent in 1950, 78 per cent in 1960, and to over 85 per cent in 1967.[+]

Validations might be characterized as being either *central* or *local*, depending upon whether they are conducted by the research organization or by the local supervisor. Central validations, normally originating in distant cities, have been conducted, until recently, almost entirely by mail. Local validations have been conducted primarily by telephone.

With the emergence of the local supervisor, there was a trend from central to local validation. When central validations are conducted by mail, the return of postcard questionnaires is likely to be well under 50 per cent of the respondents sampled, whereas local validations by telephone reach a much higher proportion of the respondents selected for validation. Also, telephone validations can provide more information than can postcards.

In 1961 a relatively economical long distance service known as WATS Lines (Wide Area Telephone Service) was introduced. This service makes possible long distance calls at relatively low rates. The WATS Lines provide an advantage for large firms with branch offices throughout the country and for firms that contact customers throughout the country. Such firms use the WATS Lines during business hours. Since many of them have unlimited service for their WATS Lines, these lines are available after business hours and on weekends without additional cost. By 1965 the WATS Lines were being used for central validation by research departments in firms that had installed such lines for communication with branch offices.

Central validation by WATS Lines revealed the relative ineffectiveness of central validation by postcards. Although some level of fabrication had been accepted as "unavoidable" in the past, central validation by WATS Lines revealed that the level of fabrication was higher than anticipated.

In 1966 there was extensive publicity to the high level of fabrication and to validation as a means for controlling fabrication. This had the effect of equating validation with good research. Firms soon emerged that were organized for the sole purpose of providing central validating services by WATS Lines. Central validation has been concentrated during evening hours when WATS Lines are available and the proportion of "at homes" are high.

[+] Estimates obtained from the Business Research Division, American Telephone & Telegraph Company, New York.

Throughout the years validation practices have been taken for granted and the need for validation has not been questioned. Today supervisors conduct validations of at least 10 per cent of the interviews for each assignment as a responsibility covered in their supervisory fees. Supervisors have grumbled about some of the prepared introductions to validation interviews and to some of the validation questions required by some clients—introductions and questions that, to some, implied distrust of the interviewer and tended to instill in respondents a distrust of interviewers. More recently, supervisors have also become concerned about central validations by WATS Lines taking place at unreasonable hours.

EXPLORATORY STUDY INTO UNDESIRABLE VALIDATION PRACTICES

An exploratory study was undertaken by the writer to obtain indications of the prevalence of calls at unreasonable hours. Questionnaires were mailed to 76 local supervisors. These were individuals who specialized in providing supervisory field services within their own community and who were reputed to be above the clerical level.

Of the 76 supervisors to whom questionnaires were sent, 53 (70 per cent) from 49 metropolitan areas, answered the questionnaire. Although this sample is small, the 53 individuals who participated in this research may be assumed to constitute a relatively large segment of the total number of local supervisors well above the supervisory clerk level (I estimate the number of such local supervisors to be under 100). Of these 53 supervisors, 23 were from cities of over 1,000,000 population, 13 were from cities of 500,000 to 1,000,000 population, 16 were from cities of 250,000 to 500,000 population, and 1 was from a city of 100,000 to 250,000 population.

Validation Calls at Unreasonable Hours

The following question was asked: "Have any instances come to your attention in which validation calls were made at unreasonable hours?" Twenty-four supervisors, from 24 different cities, answered affirmatively.

15 supervisors, representing cities from all sections of the country, reported validation calls that took place at approximately 11 P.M. or later;

9 P.M. was the earliest evening hour mentioned as unreasonable for validation calls; and

4 calls at unreasonable hours was the median number of such calls reported. The number of such calls reported ranged from 1 to "approximately" 40.

Saturday evening, Sunday morning, and Sunday evening were also mentioned as unreasonable times at which telephone validations were conducted.

Other Validation Practices Considered Undesirable

Supervisors were asked: "Are there any other validation practices which, in your opinion, tend to make respondents regret that they agreed to be interviewed?" Of the 53 supervisors, 43 answered affirmatively. Supervisors were also asked: "Are there still other validation practices that you feel are unreasonable or not good for research?" To this question, 28 supervisors answered affirmatively. The types of undesirable practices mentioned by more than 5 supervisors are presented in the table below.

Undesirable Practice	*Number of Mentions*
Overly long validations—too many questions—repeating entire interviews	28
Two or more validation calls by different individuals for the same interview	18
Cross-examining respondent—taxing recall	11
Use of incompetent—untrained—validators	10
Creating a distrust of interviewers and/or research	7
Lack of continuity—long delays between interviews and validation calls	7

Validation calls should require sensitivity and skill. The people receiving such calls had placed their trust in a stranger and had agreed to be interviewed. The time at which the initial interviews took place was convenient for respondents, but validation calls might take place at a time not as convenient. It seems important, therefore, that the validations must be worded and executed in a fashion that tends to avoid arousing suspicion, resentment, and antagonism. This implies that validating organizations require skilled validators, sensititive validation practices, and skillfully prepared validation questionnaires. Some supervisors participating in this research indicated by their comments that these requirements too frequently were not being met.

Reliability of Validations

The most frequently mentioned of the undesirable practices was "overly long validations—too many questions—repeating entire interview." Possibly, overly long validation questionnaires reflect an inability or lack of time to prepare effective shorter questionnaires. Validations might be characterized by purpose as follows:

1. *Validation of contact*—whether the respondent was in fact contacted?
2. *Validation of interview administration*—how was the interview conducted—were the required interview aids, such as Question Cards and Exhibits, used?

3. *Validation of content*—was the information reported accurate?

There seems to be no justification for overly long validations. In *Interviewing in Social Research*[5] are reported the findings of several methodological studies that pertain to the reliability of the responses given by the same respondent to different interviewers at different times. These studies indicate a lack of consistency in the answers relating to factual characteristics. Discrepancies between initial and validation interviews can be due to factors not related to fabrication—if this is true for factual questions, it is even more likely to be true for questions involving recall or opinion.

The reliability of validation interviews can be affected by a variety of factors, including differences between the skills of the interviewer and validator, by the effect of time on the attitudes of the respondent, by whether the initial answer to a question was influenced by preceding questions, and so on. For long validations and for validations involving entire questionnaires, it would be most surprising if there were no discrepancies between the initial and validation interviews. Assuming that validations result in the detection of discrepancies, the net effect of these discrepancies tends to be cancelled out among interviewers.

Multiple Validations

The next most frequently mentioned category of undesirable practices—"two or more validation calls by different individuals for the same interview"—implies a serious problem for research—a problem affecting all levels of research personnel. Distrust in research appears to be a communicable disease: once it affects one level or phase of research, it seems to spread. The prevalence of multiple validations is evidence of the spread of this disease. A research executive in one firm justifies the need for multiple validations by saying, "I don't trust interviewers. I don't trust supervisors. I don't trust research firms and I don't trust validation services."

An article in the Newsletter of the New York Chapter of the American Marketing Association, in which multiple validations are suggested, indicates how the present obsession with validation tends to demean research:

> Why (validate) the supervisor if it is the interviewer herself who has conducted the interview. The problem seems to lie in the loyalty of the supervisor for her interviewers.
>
> Without a check on the supervisor, it is possible for her to conceal her cheaters.

By casting suspicion on the integrity of the interviewer and the supervisor, the author does not seem to realize that he invites suspicion on higher levels of research. The research executive quoted before might rephrase the above quotation to read as follows:

---

[5] Herbert Hyman, *et al., Interviewing in Social Research* (Chicago: The Chicago University Press, 1954), pp. 243–252.

Why (validate) the research organization if it is the interviewer who has conducted the interview. The problem seems to lie in the research organization's desire to protect its reputation for the quality of its field.

Without a check on the research organization, it is possible for them to conceal their cheaters.

The present tendency seems to be in the direction of an increase in multiple validations with supervisors policing interviewers, research organizations policing supervisors, and clients policing research organizations. In the case of at least one firm's product tests, the possibility exists that nine validation calls might be made to the same respondent.

Cross-Examining Respondents—Taxing Recall

Interviewing for survey research differs from other types of interviewing in at least three basic respects:

1. *Absence of pressure to grant the interview*—the respondent is not applying for benefits or services and is otherwise not required to grant the interview;
2. *Anonymity*—there is an implicit or explicit guarantee of anonymity in survey research to respondents, whereas in other types of interviewing anonymity may or may not be assured; and
3. *Option to refuse answers*—the respondent is free to refuse answers to questions in survey research with impunity, whereas in other types of interviewing there are implicit or explicit pressures for providing answers to all questions

In survey research the use of information provided by a respondent in ways that might disturb, embarrass, or otherwise distress the respondent is contrary to the spirit in which the interview was solicited and granted. The practice of cross-examining respondents suggests a lack of sensitivity for the contract agreed upon between interviewer and respondent during the initial interview. This practice probably results in part from a lack of training or improper training of validation personnel, a lack of skill or care in the preparation of the validation questionnaire, and overly long intervals between the initial interview and the validation interview. Supervisors suggested that the personnel used for validation should have a background of training as interviewers and should be thoroughly briefed on the studies for which they conduct validations in order that they may handle the validations with understanding and sensitivity.

The Lack of Continuity—Long Delays Between Interviews and Validation

Supervisors report that respondents are being asked to report verbatim the answers they gave up to ten weeks after the initial interview took place. Obviously, if it is the function of validation to determine whether or how an interview was conducted, the validation should follow the initial interview as quickly as possible.

The long delays between initial interviews and validation calls might be designed to obtain information relating to the effects of time on the opinion and attitude of the respondent. In such cases, it is difficult to understand how discrepancies between the initial interview and the validation call can be the fault of the interviewer.

Creating a Distrust of Interviewers and/or Research

This category of undesirable practices includes references to introductions and to questions required for validations and to other practices supervisors considered demeaning to interviewers and to research. Supervisors were asked, "In the introductions used for validation, have any introductions come to your attention that contain wordings, phrases or sentences that you feel would tend to lower the respondent's opinion of the interviewers and of research?" To this question, 16 supervisors answered affirmatively. The wordings in validations to which supervisors objected were primarily:

1. Wordings that reflect on the honesty of the interviewer (i.e., "we are checking on an interviewer," or "were you interviewed?");
2. Wordings that reflect on the competence of the interviewer (i.e., "our interviewer omitted a few questions," or "she forgot to ask you"); and
3. Deliberately false statements.

Wordings that reflect on the honesty or competence of the interviewer are particularly unfortunate in the validation of product placements, since the interviewer must face the respondent on the call-back interviews. In the smaller metropolitan areas such wordings can affect the recruiting and retention of field staffs. Deliberately false statements, designed to provide an excuse for repeating questions asked in the initial interview, too frequently are recognized as falsehoods by respondents.

CURRENT STATUS OF VALIDATION

The need for validation stems from the uniqueness of the occupation. It is sound administrative practice to review and evaluate, to some degree, the work of all individuals who participate in any activity. Such reviews and evaluations are normally frequent for new additions to staff and tend to become periodic and routine for staff members who have shown the ability to cope with the tasks to which they have been assigned. When the occupation is one in which the staff can be supervised in the performance of their tasks and is one that permits a comparison of the finished product against the data or materials from which the finished product was derived, routine methods of review and evaluation are usually available. Normal types of review or evaluation cannot be used for the interviewer, since in the performance of her task she is rarely accompanied by supervisory personnel, and the number of factors that affect the interviewer-respondent relationship are such that this relationship cannot be exactly duplicated. Therefore, the review and evaluation of an interviewer's work requires a special methodology—validation.

What Can Validation Do?

The interviewer's tasks as they relate to the respondent might be grouped as being (1) contact, (2) questionnaire administration, and (3) reporting. Although it may not be possible to reconstruct the interview for purposes of evaluation by means of recontacting the respondent, it is possible to learn with a relatively high degree of accuracy whether the respondent was in fact contacted, and it is possible to learn with a lesser degree of accuracy whether various interview aids were used in the administration of the questionnaire. It seems doubtful whether the reporting can be evaluated with any reasonable degree of accuracy by recontacting the respondent. The quality of the reporting, however, can be evaluated when editing and coding takes place and the work of the interviewer is available for comparison with the work of other interviewers on the same assignment.

Differences between the initial interview and the validation interview can be due to a number of reasons not related to fabrication. For example, differences may result from clerical reporting errors in either interview, from misinterpretation of questions by a respondent in either interview, from lack of clarity in frames of reference which can result in different interpretations of a question in the two interviews, from the introductions of bias in either interview, from faulty recall on the part of the respondent, or from the lack of cooperation on the part of the respondent on the validation interview. Respondents may have various reasons for claiming they had not been contacted. It is reasonable to assume that some respondent might be called at an inconvenient time, and in order to terminate the validation interview, may claim not to have engaged in the initial interview. Some respondents may recall the length of the initial interview and may wish to avoid further involvement; some may suspect that the validation call is a sales follow-up and deny the initial contact, and so on.

Due to the lack of standards in validation, a number of questions might be raised. For example, if all other interviews for an interviewer pass the contact validation, is the interview for a respondent who denies having been contacted to be judged a fabrication? If one denial of contact is considered insufficient to categorize the work of an interviewer as passing validation, what is to be done with the questionnaire of the respondent who denies having been contacted? If three respondents interviewed by the same interviewer do not recall having been shown an exhibit, but fifteen respondents do recall such an exhibit, are the three interviews for which respondents did not recall seeing an exhibit to be judged as faulty recall or as interviews in which the exhibit was not shown?

There are instances in which validations have proven or can prove constructive, i.e., validation of new recruits to data collection and validation as used by some local field services. It is probable that among the recruits to data collection there are some who are not able to cope with the normal pressures involved in the interview situation. For such individuals the normal pressures in the interviewer-respondent relationship—pressures which should pose no problems for other interviewers—might prove demoralizing. Such individuals do not belong in data collection and it is important that those not temperamentally suited for interviewing be identified and dropped early in their careers. Present-day validation practices, central and local, assist in identifying such individuals. Some local supervisors have introduced revisions in validation practices which have demonstrated that validation can be a constructive instrument for evaluating interviewer performance and for reinforcing public good will toward interviewers and toward research.

Preoccupation with Validation Results in Neglect of Quality

The great majority of the data-collecting force is doubtlessly honest and can pass validation. However, honesty is not to be equated with quality. The honest interviewers pose problems for research that are as great, if not greater, than the problems posed by the demoralized or fabricating interviewers. It is probable that the great majority of individuals in the data-collecting field force have never received research training, and, therefore, it is probable that poor data collection practices are more damaging to survey research than is fabrication. There are doubtlessly many more poor but honest interviewers than there are habitual fabricators.

The lack of training for interviewers is probably due to the absence of a central responsibility for training in data collection. With few exceptions, research organizations do not have exclusive staffs for data collection, they use independent interviewers, supervisory clerks, or local field services when a sample design requires data collection in a community. Aside from providing instructions pertaining to the specific assignment at hand, no training in data collection is provided by such research organizations.

Lack of training is likely to increase the incidence of fabrication; the interviewer who has not been trained to cope with the variety of situations that can come up in an interview would be more likely to find certain situations demoralizing than would interviewers who have been trained to cope with them. Preoccupation with validation—a concern over basic honesty—seems to have overshadowed concern over quality in data collection.

FABRICATION IN DATA COLLECTION

By assuming fabrication to be a moral problem to be dealt with by policing, the research fraternity tends to divest itself of responsibility. Some years ago a young research executive, whose initiation involved serving an apprenticeship on the field director's staff of one of the larger research services, expressed his opinion of interviewers with this question: "Why is it that a woman who may be a pillar of her community and scrupulously honest in all other respects cheats as an interviewer?" The implication that women who agree to or decide to become interviewers might be morally strong generally, but morally weak when it comes to interviewing, is highly improbable. Yet, an assumption of this type seems to be inherent in treating fabrication as a moral problem.

Individuals in research organizations, such as field directors, project directors, analysts, and research directors, responsible individuals who are involved in planning, collecting, and processing survey data, have spoken freely of aberrations in data collection as an accepted fact of research life. Validation seems to represent a rite which provides absolution from responsibility for fabrication. If validation is conducted, then it is assumed that there is justification in using the data, even though fabrication is suspected, on the assumption that fabrication is minimal.

An alternative implication of the question raised by the young man quoted above is that there may be factors in survey research that impel fabrication. Some researchers contend that such factors are the primary causes of fabrication. In 1946, in an article entitled "The Cheater Problem in Polling," Leo Crespi said of fabrication:

> . . . the current conception of the nature of the difficulty is essentially a moral one. It will be the thesis of the present paper that this prevailing moral interpretation is shortsighted in that it engenders a narrow moralistic approach to difficulties which are fundamentally technical and only incidentally moral. The causes of so-called cheating . . . lie as much in the structure of the ballots and the conditions of administration as in the personal integrity of the interviewer. A view of the problem which highlights only the moral factor precludes the psychological perspective necessary for any effective attempt at solution . . . what is termed "cheating" is most constructively regarded as less a problem of interviewers' morals, and more a problem of interviewers' morale and the factors that make or break that morale.[6]

In his argument against the moral approach, Crespi is prophetic in his statement, " . . . since it (the moral approach) reveals a continual incidence of cheating and a more and more extensive group of the individuals who are suspects, the moral approach seems to lead only to the cynical and defeatist conclusion that everyone is a cheater."[7] He contends:

> Almost every interviewer will eventually succumb if the incitements to fabrication are made overpowering enough, if fabrication is made to appear the only practicable solution to the problems facing the interviewer. In short, if the interviewers are sufficiently de-

---

[6] Leo Crespi, "The Cheater Problem in Polling," *Public Opinion Quarterly*, Vol. IX (1945), p. 431.
[7] *Ibid.*, p. 436.

> moralized, they will fabricate. The morale concept of the problem, in distinction to the moral, counsels for solution not so much detection of the fabrication, but prevention of the demoralization.[8]

Crespi's thesis that fabrication is primarily a question of morals is supported by a methodological study reported in Hyman's book on *Interviewing in Social Research*. In that study, 15 interviewers were assigned a number of interviews, and among the respondents assigned to each interviewer was "planted" a "punctilious liberal" and a "hostile bigot." The punctilious liberal was assigned "the role of being a difficult but friendly respondent—a person incapable of giving an unqualified categorical response to any question." The hostile bigot was assigned "the role of being hostile, uncooperative and suspicious of the entire situation. He generally required considerable persuasion to answer any question at all and was on the whole vicious to the interviewer." Whereas there was relatively little fabrication in the interviews with the punctilious liberal, every interviewer fabricated at least once in the hostile-bigot interview.[9] The author states: "The greater extent of cheating in the more stressful bigot situation was clearly a function of the need to cheat in order to escape a painful situation as early as possible."[10]

Quotas, Deadlines, and the Interviewer Day

Available evidence suggests that demoralizing pressures are a major factor in the fabrication of data in survey research. Demoralizing factors might be classified as pressures due to acts of commission and pressures due to acts of omission. Among the most serious pressures due to acts of commission are overly tight deadlines, overly tight quotas, and the use of the *Interviewer Day*. Pressures due to omission result primarily from lack of training.

Let us first consider the demoralizing pressures imposed by overly tight deadlines, overly tight quotas, and the use of the Interviewer Day. These three types of pressures tend to be incorporated by research organizations in data collection assignments for administrative consideration. These demoralizing pressures are probably most responsible for fabrication in data collection. It also seems probable that these pressures can be corrected easily and quickly by the research organizations interested in curtailing fabrication. Understanding the destructive nature of the Interviewer Day requires the realization that interviewing is primarily a leisure-time activity. With relatively few exceptions, interviewers are housewives whose responsibility to children, husband, and home takes precedence over their responsibilities as interviewers. They become interviewers rather than take more lucrative employment that offers such fringe benefits as sick leave, vacations, and the like, not available to them as interviewers, because they cannot commit

---

[8] *Ibid.*
[9] Hyman, *op. cit.* pp. 238–241.
[10] *Ibid.*, p. 242.

themselves to the fixed schedule of hours called for by regular full-time or regular part-time employment. Many data collection problems, including fabrication, stem from ignoring the fact or being ignorant of the fact that, with relatively few exceptions, interviewers are not available or cannot be available on a fixed-time schedule—cannot afford and cannot regularly abide by the 7 or 8 hour Interviewer Day. Yet the Interviewer Day represents a pressure to which interviewers are normally required to agree in order to obtain interviewing assignments.

The Interviewer Day is important at the research planning level. It provides a unit which can be useful in estimating budgets and schedules. But, since relatively few interviewers can regularly provide 7 or 8 hours a day, the use of the Interviewer Day at the data collection level represents a serious potential for demoralizing interviewers. The interviewer might occasionally neglect her priority responsibilities, but she cannot be expected to forego them regularly or frequently. Therefore, the use of the Interviewer Day begs for aberrations—begs for shortcuts that will permit the interviewer to carry out her primary responsibilities and at the same time appear to meet the "unreasonable" time commitment imposed upon her. Deadlines are set with the Interviewer Day in mind; quotas are set with the Interviewer Day in mind; and, what is demoralizing for the supervisor, interviewing materials, exhibits, and interviewing aids are sent to the supervisor with the Interviewer Day in mind.

Lack of interviewer training must be recognized as an important demoralizing pressure. A Committee of the American Marketing Association, in a report on the training of field interviewers, made the following statements in 1948:

> There is a keener need for training interviewers because of the conditions under which they work. When an interviewer works, he is farther removed from supervision than is true of most workers. Also, he is faced with the necessity of selling himself to the respondent within a few minutes. In order to do this effectively, the interviewer must be well grounded in the general principles and techniques of interviewing as well as in the instructions and procedures for that particular survey—in other words, he must have been trained.[11]
>
> Without well-chosen, well-trained, accurate, intelligent, and conscientious interviewers, the ablest home office staff with the best conceived plan for a field investigation is futile. Even worse, the 'facts' collected by inferior interviewers may be more misleading in making decisions than would the lack of facts.[12]

The better trained the interviewer, therefore, the more likely she is to respond quickly and effectively in the new situations with which she is

[11] Committee on Marketing Research Techniques, American Marketing Association, *op. cit.*, p. 372.
[12] *Ibid.*, p. 377.

constantly faced. Interviewers who have received little or no training might find demoralizing the pressures of interview situations that trained interviewers can take in stride. The new interviewer who has not received thorough training might start fabricating early because routine pressures, which could be neutralized by training, prove demoralizing in the absence of training.

Interviewers who have received adequate training are provided with a background of information designed to provide them with an understanding of research and a respect for their data-collecting functions. Such interviewers can be expected to conduct their assignments with greater fidelity to the research design than interviewers without adequate training. As one researcher puts it, "Much of the cheating, I believe, is the result of ignorance on the part of the interviewer on the genuine importance of absolute honesty."[13]

A local supervisor of high integrity contends that much fabrication might come under the heading of "innocent cheating"—fabrication based upon innocence of the effects of aberration and based upon an improper interpretation of her role. Untrained or badly trained interviewers, who have been left with the impression that the number of interviews they provide is more important than the quality of the data they collect, can be expected to take shortcuts with what they consider to be unimportant in order that they might carry out what they consider to be their principal responsibility—making their quotas within the time allowed to them. The demoralizing pressures that tend to be operative in data collection might be classified as follows:

1. *Client-imposed Administrative Pressures* include high quotas, tight deadlines, piece rates, the Interviewer Day, and the like;
2. *Sample Design Pressures* include undesirable or "dangerous" neighborhoods, locating respondents with rare or improbable characteristic combinations, etc. (sample design pressures can be most demoralizing when combined with administrative pressures);
3. *Questionnaire Design Pressures* include the use of techniques or shortcomings in questionnaire construction that present difficulties in administering, irritate respondents, or are beyond the comprehension of respondents;
4. *Supervisor-imposed Administrative Pressures* are similar to the Client-imposed Pressures and occur when the supervisor or supervisory clerk assumes the function of foreman;
5. *Self-imposed Pressures* result when the interviewer agrees to the hours required for an assignment and these hours conflict with the time required for priority responsibilities (this category of pressures might also include the Interviewer Day);
6. *External Pressures* include weather conditions, road conditions, and the like;

[13] Gordon M. Connelly in "Survey on Problems of Interviewer Cheating," *International Journal of Opinion and Attitude Research* (September, 1947), p. 100.

7. *Lack-of-Training Pressures* include the situations that occur during an interview for which the interviewer has not been properly prepared through training—situations that pose demoralizing problems to the untrained and are not problems to the trained.

If fabrication is exclusively a moral problem, then an organized system of policing such as that proposed by FACT[14] and an increase in central validation might prove effective in limiting fabrication. If, however, fabrication is to an appreciable degree a morale problem, then an increase in policing that is not accompanied by attention to the correction of demoralizing factors might prove successful in identifying errant interviewers, but have little success in limiting fabrication, and might in fact have undesirable consequences. At a time when the need for data collection keeps increasing and at a time when the recruiting of interviewers keeps becoming more difficult, increased policing, particularly if it is effective, combined with creeping demoralization, may give rise to serious staffing problems.

To properly understand the conditions and factors that demoralize interviewers and tend to impel fabrication, it is necessary to understand the background and composition of the personnel involved in data collection —the interviewers, the supervisors, and the field directors.

INTERVIEWERS

Considering the relatively low hourly pay that is the rule for interviewing, it is not likely that those who choose to become interviewers do so because of the salary. The most attractive features of interviewing are the flexibility of hours and the freedom to accept or reject assignments. In exchange for this flexibility, the housewife is willing to accept the relatively low hourly rates available for data collection. It is probable that interviewing is the most attractive of the occupations in which she can use the time segment she has to offer. The income derived from interviewing, with relatively few exceptions, is auxiliary or supplementary income—income that might contribute toward the purchase of a new car, the purchase of a new refrigerator, sending a child to private school, and so on. Some interviewers are careful to prevent their aggregate total income from exceeding the level which might affect their status as dependents.

Interviewing, being related to research, is a prestigeful occupation and can be, clients permitting, interesting, challenging, and satisfying. For the most part, the more intelligent and more energetic housewives in the community tend to be attracted to interviewing. These are women who either have some incentive to work or are too energetic to be content to stay at home and vegetate. The more responsible of the new interviewers who find that the demand on their time interferes with their priority responsibilities tend to be forced out of the field. The less responsible interviewers tend to

[14] Advertising Research Foundation, Inc., "Progress Report on FACT," May 9, 1967.

develop shortcuts, evasions, and other practices which permit them to continue as interviewers without serious infraction on their priority responsibilities.

It seems reasonable to assume that relatively few, if any, recruits have a predisposition to cheat or have intentions of biasing or undermining the value of the data they would collect. Fabrication is likely to be due either to demoralizing pressures encountered during the interview or due to "common sense" applied under stress when the interviewer has not had the training necessary to know what is right.

Today, the interviewing personnel available in a community might be divided into three categories as follows:

1. *Independent Free-lance Interviewers—the Interviewer Pool*—are interviewers who are not affiliated with and, therefore, not responsible to, any single individual or firm in their communities. They make known their availability for interviewing to any individual or firm that uses interviewers. Some make their availability known only to sources of assignments within their community, and others make known their availability to firms such as advertising agencies, research companies, and field services outside their community. Since no single individual or organization bears responsibility for these individuals, relatively few have received formal training.
2. *Staff Interviewers Not Subject to Local Control* are resident interviewers who tend to devote the time they spend interviewing to the assignments of a single organization—an organization with headquarters in a distant community. Many of these interviewers are likely to have received training in the type of interviewing conducted by the firm with which they are affiliated. The supervision they receive on particular assignments is normally by mail or by telephone; they are not accountable for their work to any local individual. Some of the firms employing such interviewers have traveling supervisors who periodically visit their staff interviewers.
3. *Staff Interviewers Subject to Local Control* are interviewers who tend to devote the time they spend interviewing to the assignments of a single local supervisor—a local field service. All the interviewers in this category are likely to have received some amount of interviewer training. The interviewers in this category are likely to be protected by their local supervisors against client-imposed demoralizing pressures.

Fabrication in data collection in any community is likely to be concentrated among the interviewers in the *Interviewer Pool*. These interviewers are likely to be untrained, are likely to be production oriented, are seldom held accountable for their innocent or deliberate interviewing sins, are exposed to conflicting requests for their interviewing time, and are not accountable to any single local individual. Unfortunately, in most cities the Interviewer Pool represents the majority of the available interviewing personnel.

There are relatively few *staff interviewers not subject to local control* in any community. Some research organizations use only staffs of this type. The interviewers in this classification today are likely to be local representatives of research organizations that use probability samples. Only those research organizations that use the same primary sampling area for a number of studies are likely to have this type of staff.

The *staff interviewers subject to local control* are likely to be the exclusive staffs of local field services that refuse to entrust their reputations to the interviewers from the Interviewer Pool. The interviewers in this classification represent a relatively small but growing proportion of the data collection personnel.

The great majority of research organizations depend upon the talents of the Interviewer Pool or the talents of staff interviewers subject to local control. Sampling requirements for most research firms call for the availability of staff in a large number of communities throughout the country, but do not permit the constant use of such staffs. Studies conducted by most research organizations are likely to vary greatly in their sample designs. Each study is likely to call for a different set of sampling points. The frequency with which a community is used, therefore, would vary with the sampling needs of the studies contracted for by the research firm. A research firm may use some cities frequently and others infrequently. The staff of one city might be used repeatedly for a number of months and then not used over an extended period of time. Consequently, with very few exceptions, it does not pay for research firms to invest in the training of staffs for the communities that fall into their samples. Most research firms, therefore, have a file of names of available independent free-lance interviewers or local supervisory services on whom they call as the need requires. Since the use of local field services increases the cost of data collection, many research firms prefer to employ the independent free-lance interviewers.

SUPERVISORS

Today, the word supervisor is used loosely to include any individual who can supply the services of one or more interviewers in her community. In the early years of research, a supervisor was usually an employee of a single research organization. He or she acted as an interviewer on small assignments and was responsible for recruiting, training, and administering others when an assignment called for more than one interviewer. Today, nearly all interviewing conducted under local supervision is conducted by independent supervisory personnel whose services are available to any research organization—supervisory personnel who are not the employees of any single research organization.

During the early years many research organizations exchanged names of interviewers. A research organization that required an interviewer in a distant community in which it had no field representative would call other research organizations to learn whether they might know of interviewers they would recommend in that community. In this way, interviewers began to supply services to more than one research organization and the Free-lance Interviewer emerged.

When a research organization had an assignment which required more than one interviewer in a community, the interviewer in that community would be encouraged to recruit other individuals who would agree to interview. In time free-lance interviewers began to recruit others when they received assignments from more than one research organization. As the volume of interviewing increased, there developed a need for local personnel who could provide interviewers and assume responsibility for the administration of data collection in their own communities. To fill this need, Supervisory Clerks emerged. The task of these individuals consisted mainly of making available personnel to whom they distributed and from whom they gathered data collection assignments. Today, there are probably several thousand such individuals throughout the country to whom the "supervision" of research assignments are entrusted.

From among these supervisory clerks, there began to emerge Supervisors who assumed, in addition to clerical functions, assorted functions necessary to assure quality in data collection. The steady increase of the volume of field work makes it profitable for these supervisors to invest in the recruiting and training of exclusive data collecting staffs and makes it profitable for them to concentrate their activities within their own communities—to set up Local Field Services. Such local field services started to become a factor in data collection in the early 50's.

The types of supervisory personnel now involved in data collection within communities may be classified as follows:

1. *Supervisory Clerks* are individuals who supply data collecting personnel as needed for as many research organizations as will use their services. Their supervisory functions tend to be restricted primarily to distribution and collection of field assignments.
2. *Local Field Services* are provided by Independent Local Supervisors who supply data collecting personnel as needed for as many research organizations as the size of their staffs permit. They differ from the Supervisory Clerk in that they assume a wider range of supervisory functions including the recruiting and training of staffs.
3. *Resident Supervisors* are individuals who provide supervisory services for a single research organization. They are likely to have as members of their staffs the Resident or Staff Interviewers of the organization they serve.
4. *Regional Supervisors* are individuals who are likely to serve a single research organization. Their responsibilities include recruiting, training, and retraining Staff Interviewers within a cluster of states or a region.
5. *Regional Coordinators* are individuals who are likely to work for a single research organization. Their responsibilities tend to be restricted to recruiting interviewers in a cluster of states or within a region, as

the sampling needs of the research organization employing them may require.

Supervisory Clerks represent the bulk of the supervisory personnel currently being used in data collection. These supervisors are not likely to have staffs of their own; they are likely to use the Interviewer Pool or the Free-lance Interviewers in their communities. The staff they use may vary from assignment to assignment. They owe no allegiance to the interviewers they use and in turn the interviewers owe no allegiance to them. Consequently, they have no incentive to invest in the recruiting and training of staff; they use "experienced" interviewers. As users of the Interviewer Pool, the supervisory clerks are probably responsible for nearly all fabrication and other undesirable interviewer practices in data collection in which supervisory personnel are involved. As clerks, they do not question and pass on to interviewers any demoralizing pressures imposed by clients. As foremen interested in production, they might add demoralizing pressures not imposed by clients.

The Local Supervisors with Local Field Services tend to differ from the supervisory clerks in the degree of concern they show for the quality of the data they collect. Therefore, they assume functions ranging from the recruiting and training of interviewers to the methodical control of the quality of the work turned out by their staff. These supervisors tend to be careful of their reputations and, therefore, watch carefully the work of their staffs. With such supervision, it is not so much a question of whether an interview was done, but more a question of how well it was done. To protect their investment in their staffs, these supervisors tend to protect their staffs against unreasonable deadlines, unreasonable quotas, and other unreasonable pressures. The supervisors in this category, at a rough guess, might account for 15 per cent of the data collection volume supervised locally.

The most promising development in data collection has been the emergence of Local Supervisors with Field Services. These supervisors, by limiting their attention to one community, function effectively as experts in their areas. By limiting their attention to one community, they are likely to have a thorough knowledge of the community, and, by limiting their attention to a staff under their day-to-day supervision, they are likely to have a thorough knowledge of the competence and capabilities of each member of their staffs. Consequently, independent supervisors with local field services seem best equipped to provide competent staffs and expert administration for data collection assignments. These supervisors are self-made specialists in data collection.

The Resident Supervisor, the Regional Supervisor, and the Regional Coordinator are likely to be employed by research organizations that specialize in large-scale studies and in probability samples. The resident supervisor and the regional supervisor are likely to be employed by research organizations with a relatively-low turnover in data collecting staffs. The regional coordinators are likely to be employed by organizations with a relatively high turnover in their data-collecting staffs.

When research organizations started to pass on to local supervisors the responsibility for validations by telephone, a number of supervisors rebelled at the negative impact of validation introductions and wordings that cast suspicion on interviewers and on research. They introduced changes in wording that achieved the purposes of validation and at the same time tended to reinforce rather than undermine the good will of respondents toward survey research. Other supervisors saw in validation a means for evaluating interviewer performance. For some, validation has become an indispensable tool.

The quality of interviewer personnel depends upon whether the emerging supervisors look to the talents of the Interviewer Pool or whether they develop staffs of their own. In the absence of literature, guidelines, and standards, the development of competent supervisors who might make constructive contributions to the data collecting needs of a community is now being left to chance.

FIELD DIRECTORS

Field Directors who impose unreasonable quotas, unreasonable deadlines and enforce the Interviewer Day are probably more responsible for fabrication and other data collection aberrations than any other individuals in survey research. Although they may not be the authors but simply the transmitting agents or mail clerks for others who dictate demoralizing pressures, these field directors are not absolved from being accessories to such pressures. The title field director carries with it responsibility for the collection of data within the frames of reference intended for the research. Field directors frequently are also responsible for undesirable validation practices which tend to demean data collection personnel and research. Since they contribute to some of the major problems in research, it seems obvious that field directors might most easily and most quickly correct the data collection problems for which they tend to be responsible.

Not so many years ago it was fashionable for certain types of firms to show a Director of Research in their roster of employees. This title in the past was frequently given to librarians and occasionally to other personnel not as closely related to research. Today, for certain types of firms, it is fashionable to have a Field Director. One research firm is known to have given that title to a typist for a brief period while trying to locate a more qualified person. Normally, the title of Field Director is given to the individual in a research organization—a research department or a research service or a research supplier—who is responsible for distributing data collection assignments. In the absence of standards and guidelines for this position, the job description of a field director, in terms of range of responsibility and range of authority, may vary considerably from research organization to research organization. We might identify as the primary task of the field director worthy of the title the obtaining of data that satisfy the designs of the research to which the data pertain—to provide data likely to be within the frames of reference intended by the designers of the research.

There are a number of outstanding field directors who have made a career of directing field, but these outstanding individuals represent a small proportion of the personnel classified as field directors. Many of the earlier research firms did not consistently have a sufficient volume of research to warrant having someone specialize in the direction of field. As the volume of data collection increased, the specialized occupation field director appeared in increasing numbers of research organizations, in research departments of advertising agencies, in research firms, and in the research departments of the organizations that employed field.

Since 1950, since the number of research organizations began to increase rapidly, the need for field directors has increased. In the absence of specialized training for field directors, this position tended to be filled by individuals just out of school with degrees necessarily unrelated to the position and by individuals who served brief apprenticeships under field directors in research organizations. Too often they have little or no understanding or interest in data collection in relation to the individuals or functions involved and to the sociological and psychological factors that pertain to interviewing. Such individuals are not likely to realize the impact of their behavior on the research that passes through their departments. Many who do learn by trial and error are advanced or leave research and do not remain long enough "to complete their education" and are not likely to be adequately equipped to train their successors.

Field directors might be classified as being primarily quality-oriented, convenience-oriented, or cost-oriented.

1. *Quality-Oriented Field Directors* are likely to show concern for the competence of the data collecting staffs they use. Consequently, they are likely to seek out and use the local field services with supervisors who respect research and have the ability to instill a respect for research in the members of their staffs. These field directors, to the extent that their workloads permit and their employers cooperate, participate in data collection. They are likely to have gotten to know well the supervisors they use and are likely to have knowledge of the size, competence, and versatility of staffs.
2. *Convenience-Oriented Field Directors* are likely to work with supervisors who are readily available to them whenever they call and, at the same time, have demonstrated an ability to meet deadlines consistently. They are likely to avoid supervisors who turn down assignments for whatever reason—whether the reason be that their staffs happen to be committed, that the size of a particular assignment would overtax staff, that the administrative requirements for the assignment might demoralize staff, etc. They are also likely to avoid supervisors who do not accept their specifications and instructions without question—the "trouble makers." In short, their requirements are not so much quality as they are ready availability, acquiescence, and promptness.
3. *Cost-Oriented Field Directors* are likely to avoid supervisory fees

and, therefore, prefer to use free-lance interviewers whenever possible. When they have need for supervisors, their criteria for selection is likely to be cost and convenience. They are very like the convenience-oriented field directors but are more cost conscious.

When the convenience-oriented or cost-oriented field directors use supervisors, they are likely to use supervisory clerks.

Fieldability

To evaluate the effects of field directors on data collection and to understand better what the position entails, it is necessary to introduce the term *fieldability* in connection with research designs. A field director should have sufficient background and experience to judge whether the various elements in a data collection assignment are fieldable: whether the questionnaire, the techniques incorporated in the questionnaire, and the sample design can be administered in the field, whether the information required by the research can be collected within the frames of reference intended by the designers of the research, and whether the deadlines, quotas, and other administrative requirements are compatible with fieldability. A research project may be considered to lack fieldability when anything in the design or the administration of the research affects its validity, i.e., introduces elements into the research that do not permit the research instruments to measure what they were designed to measure. Obviously, such things as techniques that cannot be carried out in the field, pressures that demoralize interviewers, and questionnaires that demoralize respondents can affect the fieldability of a research project and either limit or destroy its value.

If a field director is to prevent the design of a research project from becoming distorted, she should be equipped to perform as follows:

1. She should have the qualifications and experience necessary to pass upon the fieldability of sample designs, questionnaires, and the techniques incorporated in questionnaires.
2. She should have a knowledge of the capability and the capacity of the staffs available in the communities she uses for data collection.
3. She should control the volume of work and the schedule of work sent to various communities to avoid the consequences of overtaxing staffs.
4. She should have sufficient security and flexibility to make changes in the details of a design when necessary—when unique local conditions require changes. She should have sufficient background and knowledge to make sure that such changes do not violate the overall design.
5. She should have an awareness of what constitutes reasonable workloads for interviewers by type of assignments and should avoid demoralizing pressures in the administration requirements for field assignments.
6. She should have the background and experience necessary to pass on

whether specifications and instructions for an assignment are adequate to provide data within the frames of references intended by the designers of the research.

In order for a field director to be effective in minimizing aberrations in data collection, she must have sufficient authority in her research organization to have a veto power or to require review when anything in a research project, in her opinion, may not be fieldable. Without such authority, the field director tends to be a mail clerk rather than a responsible research specialist.

Let us consider the extreme case of a newly appointed field director with no previous experience. She starts with a file of names she inherits from her predecessor; this file constitutes her field staff. Her tasks include correspondence with data collection personnel; mailing to field without question the materials for assignments; forwarding without question the administrative requirements stipulated by others; policing deadlines; watching costs; and possibly, preparing specifications and instructions for assignments. The competence of the inexperienced field director is likely to be judged on the following:

1. Do the assignments go out on time?
2. Do the assignments return on time?
3. How much are the assignments costing?

It is her responsibility to see that the assignments are accepted by the data collection personnel in the cities she has been instructed to use. Supervisors or interviewers who are not available when she needs them represent an annoyance and possibly a threat to her security. Understandably, when her file offers alternatives, she would tend to prefer data collection personnel who don't say "No."

She is likely to be, or feel that she is, under constant pressure from project directors to complete the data collection phase of their projects. Consequently, she is likely to prefer the data collection personnel who are most efficient in meeting quotas and in meeting deadlines. As a protection against or to avoid pressures from her superiors, she might alter administrative instructions and tighten deadlines.

She is likely to categorize data collection personnel on cost criteria, and she is likely to lean toward data collection personnel with the lower cost-per-interview performances. She might try to impress her superiors with attempts at lowering field costs.

She is likely to avoid the use of data collection personnel who ask for clarification of specifications and raise other problems with respect to assignments. Too frequently the inexperienced and the inept field director may not have ready answers, and questions for which she does not have answers tend to embarrass. To such field directors, questions from field represent a nuisance and are potentially embarrassing and a threat to status.

Therefore, the less competent field directors tend to gravitate toward data collection personnel who are most available, most prompt, most reasonable in cost, and are least likely to raise questions about the research materials. By leaning toward data collection personnel who never reject an assignment, they may be depending on individuals who have developed ways and means of accommodating everyone; by leaning toward data collection personnel who have little trouble meeting quotas or deadlines no matter how tight, they may be depending on individuals who have developed ways and means for by-passing the law of averages; by leaning toward data collection personnel who are consistently below average on field costs, they may be depending on individuals who, at best, may not be spending sufficient time with respondents; by leaning toward data collection personnel who do not raise questions about assignments, they may be depending on individuals who will not bring serious problems to their attention and individuals who are likely to make changes in materials or designs without asking questions or bringing such changes to the attention of the field director.

It is probable that the convenience- and price-oriented field directors have a wider impact on data collection than do the quality-oriented field directors. Although it is possible that the better field directors are in the majority, it is likely that the less competent field directors have a wider range of contacts among data collecting personnel and, therefore, tend to have a greater impact than do the more competent field directors.

Field directors who are lacking in knowledge of research and ignorant of data collection personnel, data collection conditions, and data collection limitations are likely to function on the basis of "I don't care how you do it, but get it done, get it done quickly, and get it done cheaply."

The Project Director might be considered the architect of research and the Field Director the engineer responsible for the foundation (data collection) of the research. The project directors who are ignorant of the design factors that affect fieldability may specify materials that may not be suitable for their designs. Therefore, they need the support of field engineers who are equipped to advise on the compatibility of the materials and the specifications in relation to the research design. In the absence of such engineers, it is obvious that the data obtained for research projects may not conform to the frames of reference intended by the designers of research. In such instances, fabrication and poor workmanship at the data collection level might be expected. Even if fabrication might be minimized by validation, competence at the field direction level is necessary to minimize other aberrations and the poor workmanship which can pass validation.

Clients of Research and Validation

Clients are generally aware of the problems in data collection and have been as cynical and fatalistic about these problems as have been many of the personnel to whom they have entrusted their research. The present emphasis on central validation might be interpreted as a show of concern being put on for the benefit of the clients of research. Central validation seems to be offered as a substitute for quality in data collection. To the extent that clients of research are willing to accept this substitution, they must accept their share of responsibility for the conditions in data collection.

Too many clients have been more concerned with the cost of research than with its quality. Some clients actually sponsor aberrations in data collection when they ask for "bids" on their research projects. Since the overhead costs of research organizations tend to be fixed, given the same study design, the difference in cost for a research project among research organizations of comparable size would tend to be centered on differences in the cost of the data collection. When clients of research ask for bids, they must realize that the differences among the bids are likely to be based in a large measure on differences in anticipated data collection costs. Consequently, the bidding practice encourages demoralizing pressures and begs for aberrations in data collection.

It is possible that many consumers of research have no knowledge of the data collection phase of research and are in no position to evaluate the data-collecting performances of research organizations. It is possible that specialists are needed to provide assurance that data are collected by trained and trustworthy staffs. If research clients desire quality in the data they receive, they should insist on being assured of quality before the data are collected. Validation cannot assure quality.

Clients can accelerate improvement in data collection by insisting:

1. That reasonably well-trained data-collecting personnel be used;
2. That trustworthy personnel be used;
3. That competent supervision be used;
4. That the research organization to which they entrust their research have competent field directors;
5. That data collection be slowed down rather than speeded up; and
6. That no administrative demoralizing pressures be placed on data-collecting personnel.

CONCLUDING REMARKS

Central validation currently hinders rather than furthers quality in data collection. When honesty appears to be the principal goal, then quality tends to become the secondary consideration. Only when the honesty of the data collection personnel can be assumed can quality in data collection become a realistic goal. It is hardly likely that the women who become interviewers do so with a predisposition or desire to be dishonest. It would seem that an important first step in the direction of improving quality in data collection is the requirement that the demoralizing pressures which can undermine honesty be dealt with.

Validations, both central and local, can be expected to perform as good-will ambassadors to research, if the approach to the respondent emphasizes recognition of the respondent's contribution and appreciation for the respondent's cooperation and if validation is conducted by competent personnel sensitive to and capable of overcoming the negative implication of validation practices. Local validations, conducted by personnel with a knowledge of the study and of the participating interviewers, have the potential for controlling and improving quality in data collection.

The skills and talents now being applied in demonstrating that the data collected are reasonably honest might be applied more constructively to assuring that the personnel involved in data collection are thoroughly schooled in the *why* and *how* of their functions.

PART THREE

Researcher and Data

As the previous papers have made abundantly clear, the execution of a field plan for survey research cannot fail to be attended by the kinds of human error which afflict any man-made enterprise. Not every interview is conducted exactly according to plans and instructions. Not every respondent designated by a purely random process in a probability sample is actually included in the final roster of completed interviews.

Precisely because such problems exist, it has become more and more common for large-scale survey data to be weighted in order to bring the results in line with the original sampling specifications. Such statistical adjustments may be made by referring to standard population characteristics, independently established by the Census Bureau or some other acceptable source of data. Adjustments may be handled through the use of a "nights-at-home" formula in which each interview is assigned a weight proportionate to the probability that the respondent might have been unavailable on other evenings of the week.

Adjustments of this kind have been customary in survey research from its earliest days. They have become even more prevalent with the advent of the computer which makes possible more complex weighting procedures. While the purpose is to make samples more accurately representative of the population from which they are drawn, the practice of adjustment and weighting has the effect of alienating the data from the researcher. The tables that he deals with no longer necessarily mirror the original interviews. These have been transformed into numbers and percentages which bear varying relationships to the original information collected. A sample of 1,000 interviews may appear as 2,500 after the adjustments are made, and the analyst who examines and compares the results for particular subgroups of the population may have no idea as to the number of real cases that the numbers represent.

The next paper presents an authoritative explanation and defense of the adjustment procedure in large-scale survey research. The author, Lester R. Frankel, is a prominent statistician who was among the pioneer users of probability sampling in the U.S. government. He is Executive Vice-President of Audits & Surveys, Inc.

8. Are Survey Data Being Over-Adjusted?*

LESTER R. FRANKEL

The process of adjusting data is not new nor is it confined to sample survey operations. When astronomy first became a science the early workers made observations on the positions of fixed stars. It often happened that in observing a fixed star not all of the readings on the telescope were the same. Since this was no reason to believe that the star had changed position it was assumed that the discrepancies in the measurement were due to errors of observations. In order to arrive at the best estimate of the true location of the star all of the measurements were averaged and an adjusted value was derived.

The adjustment of data in everyday life is not unusual. It is very rare that a student's grade in a course is dependent upon the results of one examination. The student may do well on one test and poorly on another. If a series of tests is taken, an average grade is a better assessment of performance than relying upon only a single test. This average is an adjusted or derived value.

In all instances where data are adjusted there are certain elements in common. There is first some true, but unknown, value that we are attempting to ascertain, i.e., the position of the fixed star in the first example and the true performance of the student in the second. Second, a number of observations are made. Finally, some mathematical processing of the data is performed—in the two cases above averages are obtained—and an adjusted value is obtained. Adjustments are made in the interest of coming close to the truth.

A sample survey is essentially a procedure whereby a large number of observations are made upon a phenomenon, and derived values are obtained to describe the phenomenon.

In contrast to the illustrations cited above, a sample survey is a complicated affair. It is executed by means of internal as well as external operations. A survey starts out with the internal operations of planning the overall design so as to fulfill the objectives, designing and setting up the sample,

*Presented to the Market Research Council, December 17, 1965.

and preparing the questionnaire, the interviewer materials, and the instructions. The next series of operations is external. These include the field sampling and the actual interviewing, with its attendant control and field verification steps. Internal operations then take over when the completed questionnaires have been returned from the field.

Editing and coding operations take place, and further checking is done. The basic individual survey data are then transferred to IBM cards, put on magnetic tape, or perhaps left on the questionnaires themselves.

The next step is that of making the tabulations. It is here that the term "adjustment" is used in connection with sample surveys. Since the use of this word has been subject to a great deal of misunderstanding during the past few years, it is necessary to define it precisely and position it before the question of whether or not survey data are overadjusted can be answered.

There are two phases or aspects of the tabulation process. The first, or *synthesis* phase, is the preparation of the basic statistical estimates that the survey was designed to obtain. In an audience study, these basic estimates are the readership percentages for each magazine for the total population and for segments within. In a study of family income relating to education of the head, the basic estimates are the income distribution for various levels of education.

The second aspect of the tabulation process, the *analytical* phase, is concerned with the preparation of analytical tables and analytical devices. For example, in the case of the family income study, one can obtain correlation coefficients. One can also build into the tabulation process measures of statistical significance.

It is important for our discussion to keep the distinction between these two phases, i.e., the synthesis and analytical, in mind. The two are generally considered together because the same statistician is involved in both, the same computing machinery is often used for both, and the tabulation specifications are prepared and issued as a single document. Finally, to many people the two phases are subsumed under the collective designation, "statistical manipulation."

The phrase "adjustment of survey data" is confined to the synthesis phase, that is, the processes involved in taking data in the raw form and deriving estimates of the basic parameters involved. Depending upon the degree of sophistication of an outsider, as well as his emotions, these processes have been described as: statistical estimating, ratio estimating, adjusting, weighting, balancing, duplicating cards, juggling, massaging the data, making up interviews, and crystal gazing.

From this myriad of terms in current use to describe these processes, there are only two which are important and meaningful to the statistician. These are *weighting* and *adjusting*. Within the framework of probability sampling, they have separate and definite meanings.

Consider the term "weighting." It often happens that in the design of a sample survey, it is decided for one reason or another to make use of an unequal probability selection method. For example, the design may call for the selection of one out of every hundred upper-income households and one out of every five hundred of the remaining households. In order to obtain unbiased estimates of the population in this design, each individual observation has to be "weighted" by a number proportional to the reciprocal of the probability of selection. Thus, the upper-income households receive a weight of one and all other households receive a weight of five.

Not too many years ago, before the advent of the computer and when card-counting sorters were used to tabulate data, it was convenient to accomplish this weighting by duplicating IBM cards. Thus, one IBM card would be used for each upper-income household interviewed and five identical IBM cards (one original card plus four duplicates) would be used for each household that was not designated as upper-income. This gave rise to the belief among some people that weighting involved "making up interviews." Whether an unequal or an equal probability selection method should be used in the first place is a question outside the scope of this discussion. However, weighting is a necessary step whenever unequal probability selecting methods are used.

Now, we come to the term "adjustment." This occurs after weighting has taken place. The best definition of this term was given by Deming, many years ago who said, "adjustment is where the end product is a set of values which have been forced to satisfy certain conditions."* It is obvious that the conditions to be satisfied should be known independently of the survey. The purpose of forcing is the hope to get closer to the truth than if no forcing were done.

The following four examples illustrate the role of adjustment.

1. Three angles of a triangle are measured. When the three measurements are summed they add to more than 180 degrees. The angular measurements are adjusted so that they do add up to exactly 180 degrees.
2. According to Charles' Law, the volume of a gas is directly proportional to its temperature. Volumetric measurements are made at different levels of temperature and the points do not fall on a straight line. A straight line is "fitted" to obtain the adjusted values for various levels of temperature.
3. A nationwide sample survey is conducted in order to obtain the employment status of all persons 14 years of age and older. After tabulating the basic data, it is observed that, mainly because of non-response, the distribution of age and sex in the sample does not coincide with the already known distribution in the population. The sample is brought into line and made to agree with the population on the basis of the age-sex distribution. Then overall employment status is estimated.
4. A sample of drug stores is selected in order to estimate the volume of cosmetic sales in these outlets. From each store in the sample, dollar sales of cosmetics as well as total store sales are obtained for a given

*W.E. Deming, *Statistical Adjustment of Data* (New York: John Wiley & Sons, 1943), p. 13.

period. For the universe of all drug stores, the aggregate total sales as well as the frequency distribution of drug stores of total sales is known. The results for the sample drug stores are adjusted so as to force agreement with the known population figures for total sales of all drug stores. Then on the basis of the adjusted values, cosmetic sales are estimated.

As stated above, the purpose of adjusting is to come closer to the truth than if no adjustment were made. The basic questions are: "Do we actually get closer to the truth by making adjustments?" and "Is it possible that by making more and more adjustments we get further from the truth?" We shall see that the adjustment process can, if properly applied, accomplish its purpose. It is a very effective device. However, one should be extremely careful in making use of it. If used incorrectly, it could lead to disastrous results.

Let us first consider non-statistical pitfalls in attempting to force sample data to agree with some standard. They do not arise from the statistical handling process. They do arise because in some cases the control data that are obtained in the survey are not identical with the control information on the population. In the U.S. Census Monthly Report on the Labor Force, it has been the practice, since its inception, to adjust the survey data so that the percentage distribution of five age groupings by sex would coincide with highly accurate independent population estimates in these ten cells. Soon after the end of World War II, it became apparent that returning veterans were creating turbulence in the labor market. It was decided to split the males into two parts: male veterans and male non-veterans. Excellent information on the size and age distribution of the veteran population was obtained from official sources. In the interviewing process, the veteran status of each male in the sample was ascertained. When the sample results were being processed, it became obvious that, if the new adjustment procedure were followed, the labor force series, which had been behaving regularly up to that time, would become erratic. An investigation indicated that the definition of a veteran, according to official sources, was not identical with how the male respondent was classified. Many men still in the Armed Forces, but in a civilian status and out of uniform, were mis-classified as veterans by the enumerators.

Before any adjustment can be made, it is essential that the survey definition for the control variable be identical with the definition used for the variable in the population. If these definitions are not identical we can be worse off by making adjustments.

Now let us consider adjustments from the statistical point of view. We want to know how adjustment relates to closeness to the truth. In statistical inference we do not deal with single instances, but with expectations. So now the question becomes: "How close can I expect to be from the truth?" The closeness to truth can be expressed as a fixed value and is called the *Root Mean Square Error*. It is made up of the *sampling error* and a term called the *bias*, and they are related according to the diagram on page 93.

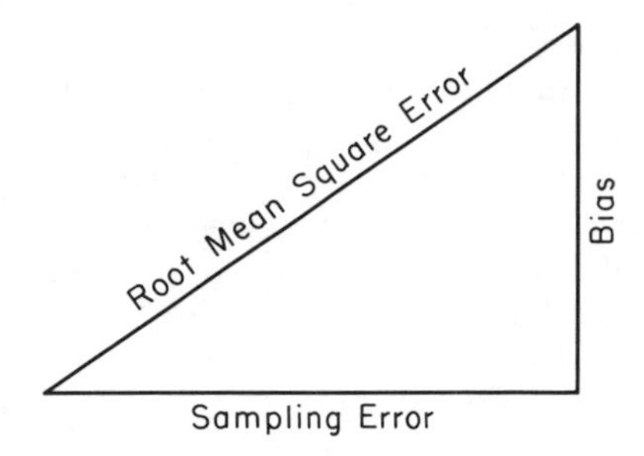

In general the time bias refers to all non-compensating errors. However, for purposes of our discussion, the bias will refer specifically to the error, if any, in a sample estimate arising because not all segments of the population receive their proper representation. The purpose of any adjustment is to minimize the mean square error. An adjustment procedure may accomplish this by reducing the bias, by reducing the sampling error, or both. It often happens, however, that by reducing one leg of the above triangle the other may be increased. As a result the mean square error may not be affected, or it may even be increased.

In order to understand the forces involved, we shall consider a hypothetical example where all of the values of the universe are known. A sample is selected, and estimates of the parameters are made using different adjustment procedures.

In Table I, below, we have a complete description of a population in terms of smoking behavior, as well as the distribution of the sample and

TABLE I
Universe

		Number of Cigarettes Smoked			*Interviews*	
Demographic Group	*Proportion*	*Average*	*Standard Deviation*	$(S.D.)^2$	*Expected*	*Completed*
Females, under 35	.25	.40	3.0	9.00	30	30
Females, over 35	.25	.50	4.0	16.00	30	30
Males, under 35	.25	.60	5.0	25.00	30	30
Males, over 35	.25	.70	6.0	36.00	30	10
					120	100
Females	.50	4.5	3.7	13.75	60	60
Males	.50	6.5	5.6	31.75	60	40
					120	100
All people	1.00	5.5	4.8	22.75	120	100

the completed interviews. The top section shows the distribution in terms of age-sex specifics. The middle section, which is derived from the top, shows the distribution in terms of sex specifics; and the bottom section, which is also derived from the top, shows the overall parameters. A sample of 120 individuals is selected, but only 100 completed interviews are actually made.

We now consider three methods for estimating the average number of cigarettes smoked per day. While the first method involves no explicit adjustment, it has the effect of distributing the 20 non-interviews among the four groups proportionate to the number of completed interviews. This introduces a bias. The sampling variance is that of a simple random sample. In this case the mean square error comes out to be .3175. The details of this procedure are shown in Section 1 of Table II.

Now, consider one type of adjustment. In the population, half are men, and the other half are women. In the sample, only 40 per cent are men, and 60 per cent are women. One type of adjustment which is commonly made is to adjust the sample (i.e., estimating procedure) so that each sex is properly represented. As a result of this adjustment, the bias is reduced, and the sampling variance is increased. When the two are combined, a smaller mean square error is obtained than when no adjustment is made. Section 2 of Table II provides the details of the computation.

Let us examine the effect of carrying the adjustment one step further. If the adjustment is made on an age-sex basis, four strata are obtained. Each of the four strata is given its proportionate share in the population, and the strata means are estimated from the sample. In this case the bias is reduced to zero. However, the sampling variance increases to such an extent that the mean square error is larger than the mean square error without any adjustment (see Section 3 of Table II).

A common type of adjustment which is often justified on statistical grounds and has great intuitive appeal is the *Ratio Estimate*. Suppose a sample survey is conducted in a city in order to determine the dollar volume of drug sales in drug stores. The total sales of all commodities in drug stores is known through U.S. Census figures or from some other source. A sample is selected, and within each of the sampled stores information is obtained for drug sales as well as for total sales. The sample findings are added, and the average drug sales as well as the average total sales are obtained. These averages are then multiplied by the total number of drug stores in the city, and estimates are obtained.

If no adjusting is done, the estimate of total drug sales is the figure obtained through the above multiplication. However, suppose it is observed that, when the average total sales in drug stores is multiplied by the number of stores, the estimate of total sales is, say, 10 per cent higher than the known figure for total sales. Since the total is 10 per cent too high, it is assumed that the estimate for drug sales is too high, and an adjustment is made by reducing this sample estimate of drug sales by a comparable amount.

In actual practice, the method of ratio estimating is used in such a

TABLE II

Three Methods of Estimation

---

1. No Adjustment—Assume 20 Non-interviews Are Randomly Distributed

A. Bias = true mean minus expected mean

$$\text{True mean} = .25(4.0)+.25(5.0)+.25(6.0)+.25(7.0) = 5.50$$

$$\text{Expected mean} = \frac{30(4.0)+30(5.0)+30(6.0)+10(7.0)}{100} = 5.20$$

$\text{Bias} = 5.50-5.20 = .30$

$(\text{Bias})^2 = .0900$

B. Sampling Variance = .2275

C. Mean square error = .2275+.0900 = .3175

---

2. Adjustment for Sex Only

A. Bias = true mean minus expected mean

True mean = 5.50

Expected mean:

$$\text{Expected mean for females} = \frac{30(4.0)+30(5.0)}{60} = 4.50$$

$$\text{Expected mean for males} = \frac{30(6.0)+10(7.0)}{40} = 6.25$$

Expected overall mean (with adjustment) $= .5(4.50)+.5(6.25) = 5.375$

$\text{Bias} = 5.50-5.375 = .125$

$$\text{B. Sampling variance} = (.5)^2\frac{13.75}{60}+(.5)^2\frac{31.75}{40} = .2554$$

C. Mean square error = .2554+.0157 = .2711

---

3. Adjustment for Sex and Age

A. Bias = true mean minus expected mean

True mean = 5.50

Expected Mean (with adjustments) $= .25(4.0)+.25(5.0)+.25(6.0)+.25(7.0) = 5.50$

$\text{Bias} = 5.50-5.50 = 0$

$$\text{B. Sampling variance} = (.25)^2\frac{9.00}{30}+(.25)^2\frac{16.00}{30}+(.25)^2\frac{25.00}{30}+(.25)^2\frac{36.00}{10} = .3292$$

C. Mean square error = .3292 + 0 = .3292

---

manner that the sample observations are used to estimate the ratio of drug sales to total sales and this ratio is multiplied by the known total sales. This method is dependent upon the correlation between drug sales and total sales. If the correlation is high, the method tends to produce highly accurate estimates. As the correlation decreases, so the accuracy decreases. With low correlations, the ratio estimating procedure will tend to yield less accurate estimates than the straight blow-up (multiplying sample averages by the number of stores) method.

Charts I and II illustrate the effects of using a simple average estimate and the ratio estimate with a sample of 50 drug stores. A measure of the accuracy of the estimate is given by the Rel. Variance, a statistical term which is a measure of the relative standard error squared. In the case of the simple average, the Rel. Variance is .00311. With the ratio estimate the Rel. Variance is .00184. In this example, the correlation coefficient between drug sales and total sales is + .69.

The adjustment procedure can be carried on to some further steps. Suppose, for example, in this city it is known that 30 per cent of the stores are small, 60 per cent are of medium size, and 10 per cent are large; and in the sample, 26 per cent are small, 58 per cent medium, and 16 per cent large. The technique of post-stratification is used whereby simple averages of drug sales for each stratum are weighted together in proportion to the distribution of stores in the population, and the adjusted average is multiplied by the number of drug stores in the city. Chart III illustrates the logic of the procedure. The Rel. Variance of this procedure is .00171.

A fourth type of adjustment can be made. This is to use the ratio estimating procedure with strata. Intuitively, it may be argued that since the ratio estimate provides more accurate data than the simple average and since the stratified sample blow-up estimate tends to be more accurate than the sample blow-up, then the ratio estimate within strata should be still more accurate. However, when Chart IV is examined, it is seen that the anticipated result is not obtained. In fact the estimate is less accurate than that obtained in Chart III and no more accurate than a simple ratio estimate.

This particular phenomenon is explained by the fact that the high correlation coefficient per cent on an overall basis is destroyed by stratifying by size of drug store. It should be recalled that the overall coefficient was +.69. After stratification, the correlation coefficients within the respective strata turned out to be +.50 for the small store strata, –.03 for the medium size stores, and –.04 for the large stores.

From these two sets of illustrations, it can be seen that the process of adjustment can sometimes lead to more accuracy and sometimes to less accuracy. Adjustment procedures must be used with care, and each use must be examined as to its implications. A statistical analysis of the steps involved related to the data on hand will often indicate the advisability of making adjustments and the extent to which they may be carried out.

Non-statistical considerations play an important role. When adjusting a sample to agree with certain population values, one should be sure that the check data obtained in the sample is by definition and execution identical with the comparable data in the population. In this respect the nature of the measuring instrument should be known before any adjustment is made. Deming cites an example where the sum of the angles of a triangle adds up to less than two right angles. If the measuring instrument (in this case the protractor) is accurate, and errors are made because of parallax, the deficit is made up by dividing it equally and adding a constant amount to each of the three angles. If, on the other hand, the protractor scale is

CHART I
Total Drug Sales

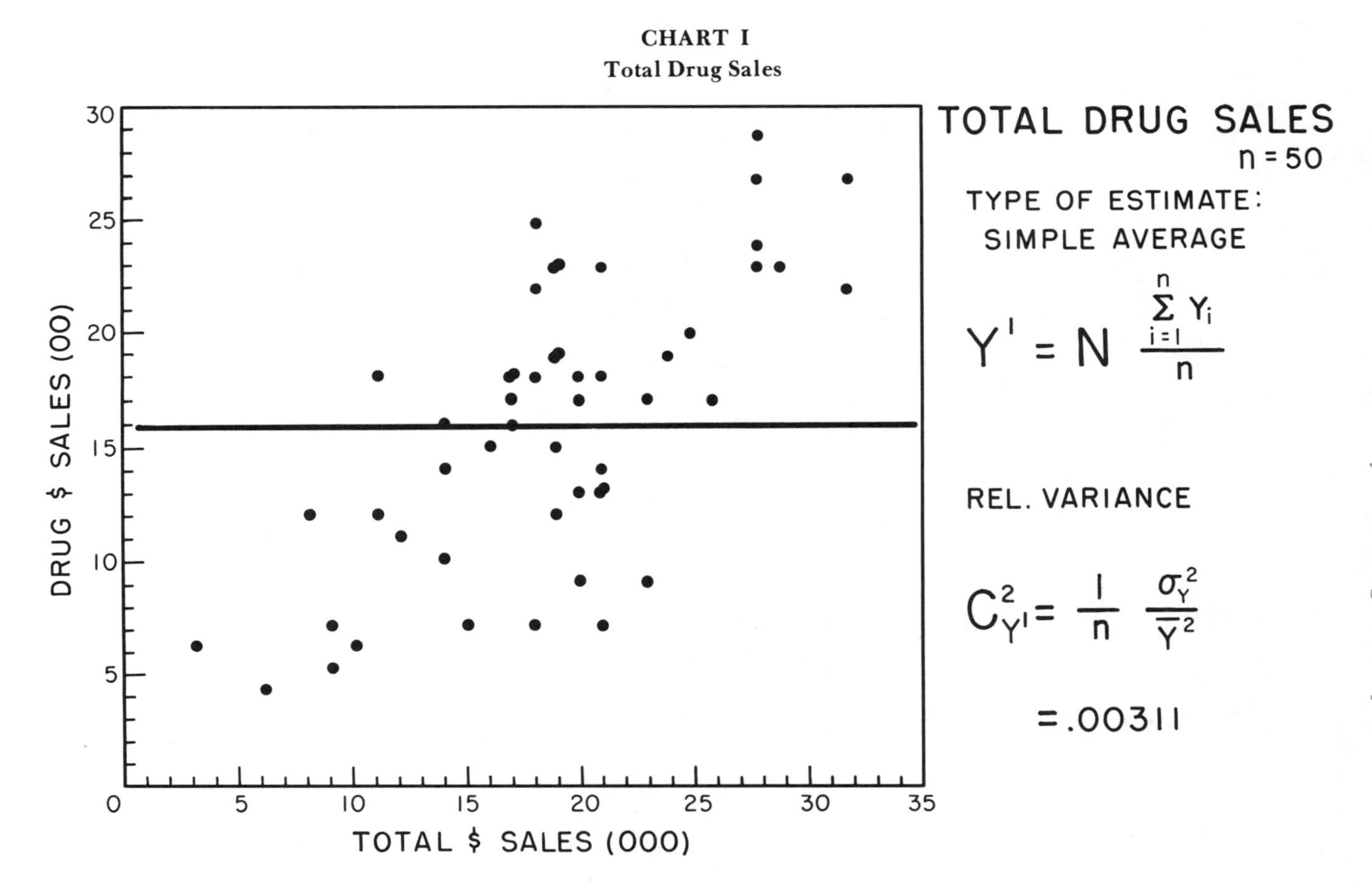

CHART II
Total Drug Sales

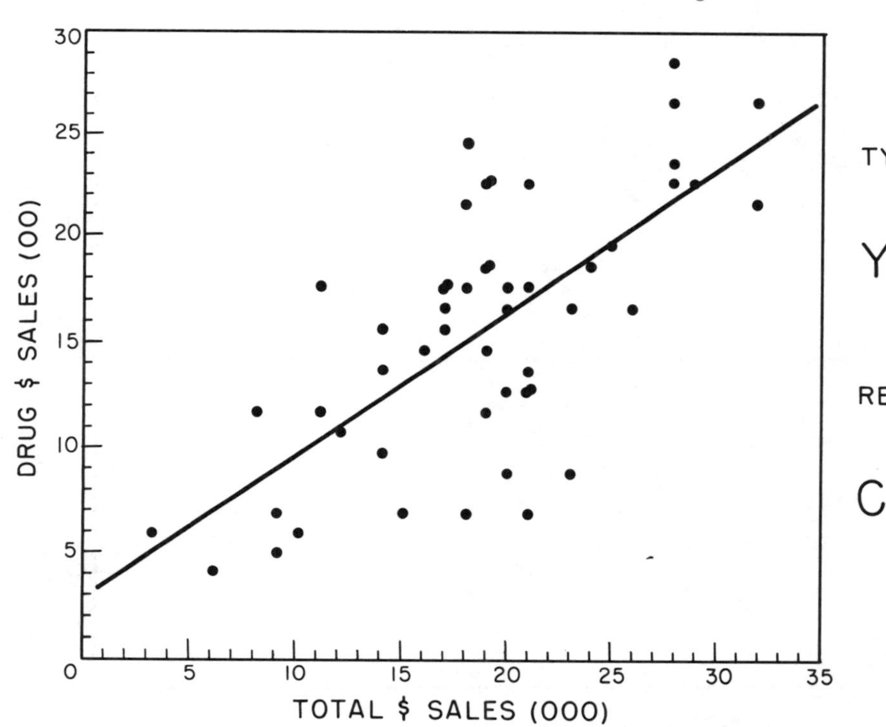

TOTAL DRUG SALES

n = 50

TYPE OF ESTIMATE : RATIO

$$Y' = X \frac{\sum_{c=1} Y_i}{\sum_{i=1}^{n} X_i}$$

REL. VARIANCE

$$C^2_{Y'} = \frac{1}{n}\left\{\frac{\sigma_Y^2}{\bar{Y}^2} + \frac{\sigma_X^2}{\bar{X}^2} - 2r\frac{\sigma_Y \sigma_X}{\bar{Y}\,\bar{X}}\right\}$$

$$= .00184$$

CHART III
Total Drug Sales

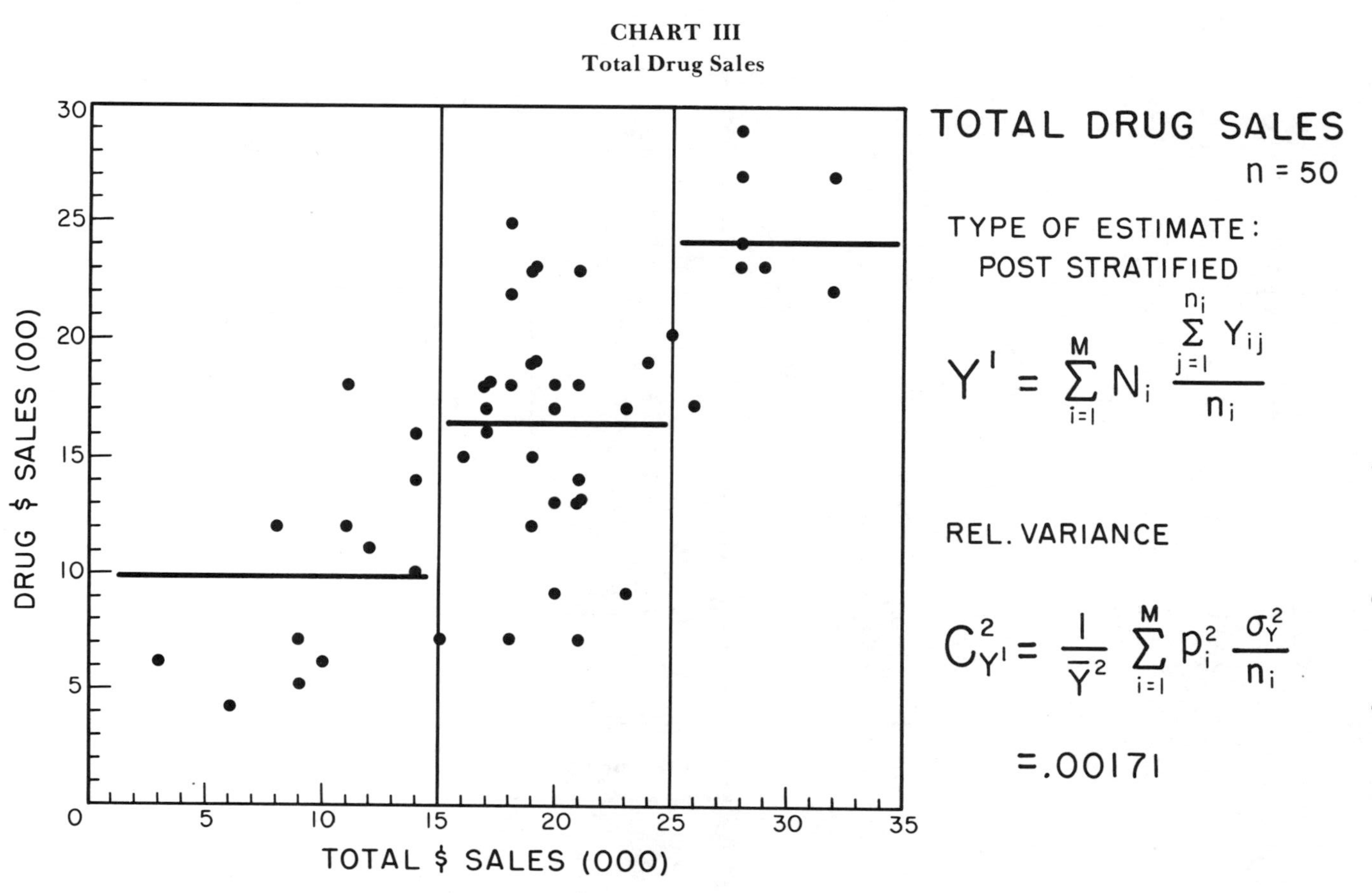

CHART IV
Total Drug Sales

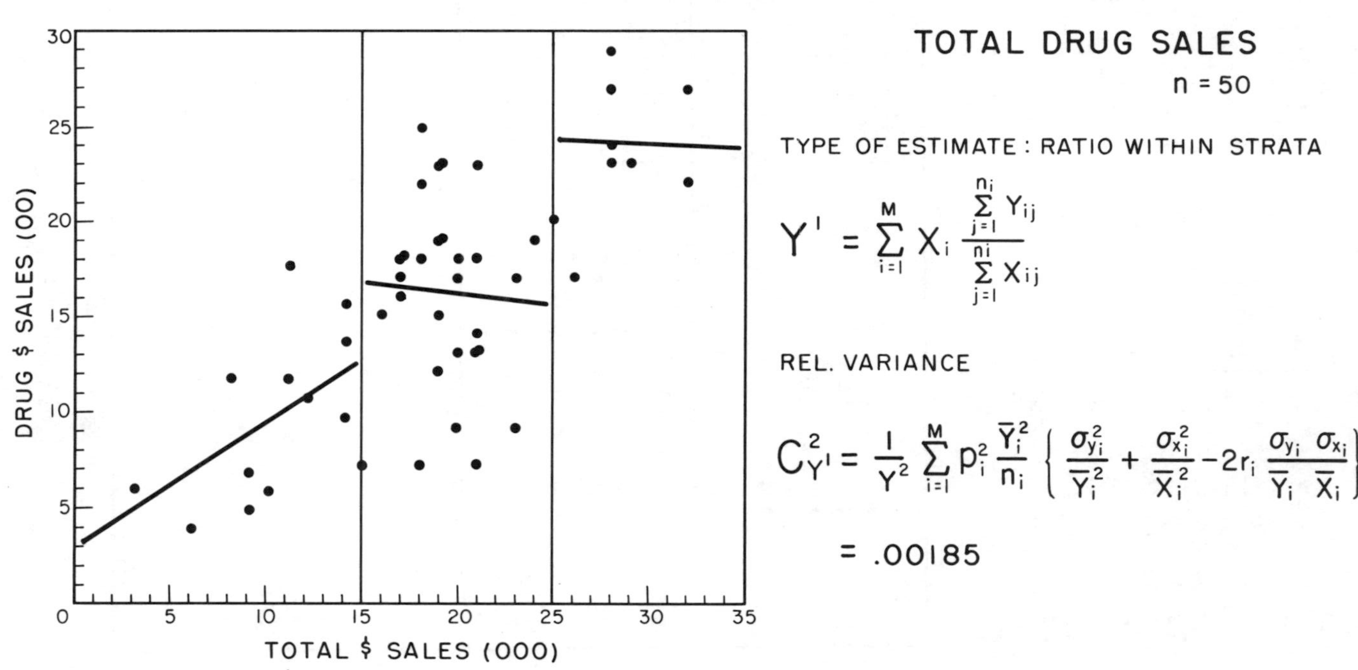

stretched and on a straight edge it reads, for example, 175 degrees, then the deficit is distributed proportionate to the sizes of the three angles that were measured.

In summing up, we see that the aim of adjusting survey data is to arrive at more accurate estimates than would otherwise be possible. While the term "adjustment" has many meanings, it has a specific meaning in the statistical sense. In making a statistical adjustment no judgment is involved in modifying, accepting, or rejecting any of the basic raw data that has been collected. The adjustment procedure that is used is applied in a predetermined mechanical procedure. There is usually a variety of adjustment procedures that may be used, and there is a definite criterion for testing the efficiency of each procedure. There are some situations where the adjustment of data may lead to less accurate results than if no adjustment has been made. A complete knowledge of the measurement process and an understanding of the estimating procedures are necessary to avoid this possibility.

The purpose of market research is always diagnostic. Even in the most simple descriptive study of consumer attitude or buying action, there is always implicitly a comparison between the usage pattern of one product and another, the market position of one brand versus its competitors, and the characteristics of people who behave one way in the market as opposed to those who take another course. To make comparisons is to state differences, and to state differences is to seek explanations.

In the following paper, Hans Zeisel, the distinguished theorist of Say It with Figures, *reviews the arsenal of methods which the researcher can employ to investigate the why and wherefore of his data. He concludes that the controlled experiment, which is the most fundamental technique of the physical sciences, also provides the basic model for analyzing causation in the kinds of social phenomena with which consumer research is concerned. Dr. Zeisel is Professor of Law and Sociology at the University of Chicago and has co-authored several significant books on the sociology of law, foremost among them,* The American Jury. *He is also Chairman of the Board of Marplan, the international research arm of the Interpublic Group of Companies.*

9. Tools of Causal Analysis*

HANS ZEISEL

The bulk of our efforts in the social sciences is still directed towards describing what is and what happens, because there are still so many areas of social behavior we have never yet seen with any precision. But more and more frequently we are also trying to find out *why* things happen and what effect they have. While description and causal analysis are seldom sharply separated, the tools of causal analysis nevertheless form a rather distinct set.

1. THE CONTROLLED EXPERIMENT

I shall begin with the glamorous tool we inherited from the natural sciences —the controlled experiment. In its simplest form, it begins with a group of people on some of whom the experiment is to be performed. The group is divided randomly, that is, by some lottery process, into two smaller groups that are for all practical purposes interchangeable *because* they were obtained through random selection. One group is then exposed to the experimental influence, while the other is not. This arrangement allows us to ascribe without hesitation any effect that appears in the exposed group, and not in the other, to the experimental influence. In the natural sciences, this is the classic experimental design for measuring, for instance, the effect of a vaccine (see Figure 1). I shall skip over the technical niceties of the experimental design; you can find them in any number of texts.[1] But I do want to add here a remark or two about the peculiar difficulties of experimenting in our field. The one concerns the obvious difficulty of experimenting with human beings. It is not by accident that some of the first of these experiments were conducted in the Army where one company could be ordered to watch an indoctrination film, while another one was used as control group.[2] Only school classes, hospitals, and, of course, prisons allow similar tight arrangements by the experimenter, and that is why the directly controlled experiment has its limits in social research.

---

*Presented to the Market Research Council, February 18, 1966.

[1] E.g., D. R. Cox, *Planning of Experiments* (New York: John Wiley & Sons, 1958); also K. A. Brownlee, "The Principles of Experimental Design," *Industrial Quality Control*, Vol. 13 (1957), pp. 1–9.

[2] Carl I. Hovland, Arthur A. Lumsdaine, and Fred D. Sheffield, *Experiments on Mass Communication*, Vol. III. of *Studies in Social Psychology in World War II* (Princeton, N.J.: Princeton University Press, 1949).

FIGURE 1

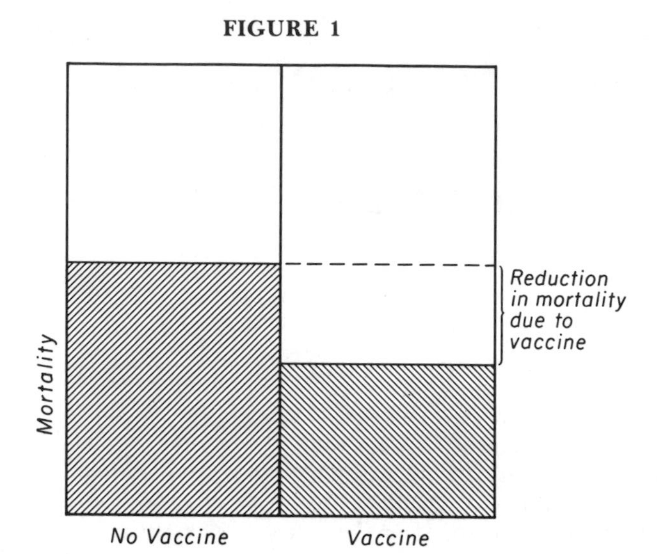

My second remark goes to the scientific yield of experiments in the social sciences. Even if feasible and even if technically precise, the insights they provide are necessarily of a limited nature. The one indoctrination film produces a measurable effect and allows of little generalization; the next film might be poor and show no effect. Here is an example from another field: that a different instruction from the judge to the jury on the law of insanity in a case of housebreaking produces different jury verdicts does not mean that it will also produce different verdicts if the case is murder.[3] This problem of generalizing exists, of course, also in the natural sciences, but the latter have a more-developed structure, hence wider generalizations are possible, and *experimenta crucis* (crucial experiments that allow broad generalizations) can be designed. The social sciences as yet lack, for the most part, such a coherent structure and also, therefore, such opportunities for broad generalizations.

2. THE SURVEY CROSS-TABULATION

I began with a discussion of the controlled experiment not only because it is, in a way, the perfect analytical instrument, but also because some of the less powerful tools of analysis are shaped after it.

The survey cross-tabulation is, on its face, indistinguishable from the tabulation of an experiment. It, too, compares those exposed to the potential cause to those who have not been exposed to it, but the comparison is made retrospectively, that is, without prior randomization of the two

[3] Rita James Simon, *The Jury and the Denfense of Insanity* (Boston: Little, Brown, 1967).

groups, and that makes a big difference. Without prior randomization, there is no way of categorically stating that prior to the experimental exposure, the two groups had been interchangeable—an indispensable requirement for ascribing the resulting effect with certainty to the exposure. The survey cross-tabulation, therefore, requires assurance that, although prior randomization is lacking, the two groups under comparison had nevertheless been originally interchangeable.

Let me first give an example in which this requirement is obviously not met. There is an old Chinese statistical joke to the effect that the people who are visited by a doctor have a considerably higher mortality rate than those who have been spared such a visit. Extreme examples have the advantage of making both the problem and the solution abundantly clear. Obviously, what is needed here is to make the Visit–No Visit comparison separately for those who prior to the event had been sick and those who had not been sick; we would then quickly find out that the latter group could safely be eliminated altogether, because it had no professional visits from doctors.

The general prescription here is to split the cross-tabulation into segments and make the exposure–non-exposure comparison separately for each of the subgroups of the total population. The question now is along what lines these subgroups should be formed. Again, the Chinese example shows the way: we must group the people in such a way that we remove whatever impeded their interchangeability prior to the exposure. Our difficulty was that practically all people in the group who had a doctor visit must have been sick, while those who had no doctor visit probably included some sick persons and also all those who had no need for a doctor. By making the comparison separately for the sick and the healthy, we remove the biasing inequality in the original group.

Incidentally, not every inequality will bias the result. If one group in the doctor example had included more redheads than the others, such inequality would not have mattered in all probability. But if one group had been older than the other, it would have, because older people would, on the whole, die sooner than younger ones. You can see that it is necessary to refine the groupings as much as possible: not only separate the healthy from the sick, but possibly also the severely sick from the other sick, the older ones from the younger ones, and so forth.

The refinement process has two natural limits: the number of cases remaining in each cell quickly becomes too small, thus vitiating any comparison; and the lack of background data might not allow further segmentation. We might know, for instance, only whether the person was sick or not, but have no information as to whether the sickness was severe or not. Therefore, to guard as least against this second limitation, it is the better part of foresight to collect in survey work all background data that could possibly help later in the analytical search.

However, the basic trouble with this procedure of fractioned analysis is that, however far it is carried, it does not guarantee cure; there is no way of knowing for sure that all the hidden factors that will render a causal inference spurious have been eliminated, however plausible the result.[4]

3. MATCHING

Another method of providing a control group retrospectively is to attempt to match those individuals who developed a certain effect with their counterparts who, under the same circumstances, failed to develop this effect. By comparing the two groups then—not with respect to the effect, but with respect to the *antecedents* of the effect—causes may be discerned.

In a most elegant inquiry designed to discover the causes of fatal automobile accidents to pedestrians, autopsies were performed on some 50 pedestrians who were 18 years old and over and who were killed seriatim in Manhattan at known sites and times. The control group was obtained by visiting the accident site on a subsequent date, but on the same day of week and hour of the day. Interviews and breath specimens for alcohol analysis were obtained from the first four adult pedestrians reaching the site who were of the same sex as the deceased. This highly original study showed that the killed came primarily from two high-risk groups: the middle-age persons who drank and the old-age bracket.[5]

4. THE NATURAL EXPERIMENT

Occasionally, we are nevertheless almost certain that retrospective data have the quality of a controlled experiment. Consider the following example. It was found that the accident rates of female drivers rise sharply during the days immediately prior and following menstruation, but interestingly enough, not so much during the period itself. Since it is very improbable that women drive during these days more frequently or in more hazardous surroundings, we are allowed to assume that nature has provided us here with a controlled experiment.[6]

5. REASON ANALYSIS

We now switch to an entirely different tool of causal research, although we shall eventually connect it with the controlled experiment: the interrogation of the actor about the motives of his actions. The method is colloquially known as the "Art of Asking Why,"[7] more technically as *reason*

[4] See "The Cross-Tabulation Explains: True and Spurious Explanations," in Hans Zeisel, *Say It With Figures* (5th edition; New York: Harper & Row, 1967).

[5] W. Haddon, Jr., and others, "A Controlled Investigation of the Characteristics of Adult Pedestrians Fatally Injured by Motor Vehicles in Manhattan," in Haddon, Suchman, and Klein (editors), *Accident Research* (New York: Harper & Row, 1964), pp. 232–50.

[6] Katherine Dalton, "Menstruation and Accidents," in Haddon, Suchman, and Klein (editors), *Accident Research, op. cit.*

[7] From Lazarsfeld's pioneering paper of that title (1935), reprinted in D. Katz, *et al., Public Opinion and Propaganda* (New York: Holt, Rinehart & Winston, 1954).

analysis. The process is complicated, and its success is limited by two facts: actions are usually the result of a very great number of different causes and motivations; and many of these motives operate unconsciously and are, therefore, difficult to find. Thus, the technique works best with respect to actions that are relatively simple and that have been taken with some deliberation. Again, an extreme example will be helpful. If a woman is asked why she switched dry cleaners, and she answers, "the old one ruined my two dresses," the answer will have the ring of completeness and truth. Even more complex consumption decisions, such as, "why did you buy this Buick Special," or "why did you go to the Bergman movie last night," will reveal satisfactory answers if the interviewer knows his job. But the more serious a decision becomes, the smaller will be the yield from asking why; "why did you vote Democrat?" is already a much more difficult interviewing subject, and to ask "why did you marry Jean?" is almost bound to be a failure.

There is no need here to go into the details of the research technique—they too are found in textbooks[8] —but it is important to show how reason analysis is related to the controlled experiment and to the cross-tabulation. Suppose we have made an indoctrination experiment by exposing a group of people to a film designed to convince them that Negroes have no innate inferiorities to Caucasians. Suppose the result of the experiment, in terms of our schematic graph, appears to be like Figure 2. We would then

FIGURE 2

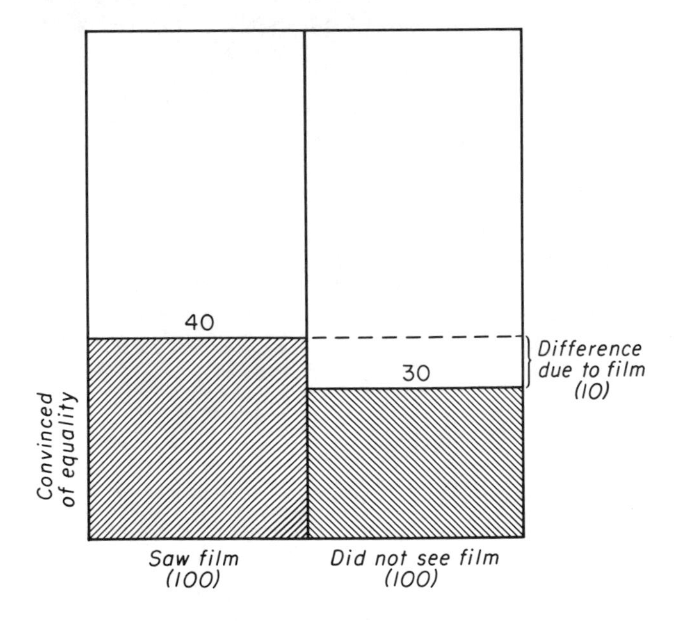

[8] See "Reason Analysis," in Zeisel, *Say It with Figures*, *op. cit.*

conclude that exposure to the film has increased the number of those convinced of the innate equality of the races from 30 to 40. The proposition that follows is that interviewing the 40 people in the experimental group as to why they believe in the innate equality of Negroes and Caucasians will elicit from ten (the difference between 40 and 30) the answer: "Because I saw a film. . . ."

It is, of course, one thing to establish the theoretical connection between the two methods of causal inquiry and quite another thing to actually reproduce it. But if the collation does succeed, it powerfully buttresses whatever findings emerge.[9]

6. REASON ASSESSMENT

There is a variant of reason analysis which it is advisable to consider separately. It has the same aim—namely to discover the structure of an individual decision process or an individual chain of events—but it does it without resorting to questioning the actor. This method is applied, for instance, to automobile or airplane accidents, where the actors are often not any longer available for questioning or, at best, conscious of only part of the total chain of circumstances. By collecting and collating all relevant clues, the analyst, who in this case must be an expert in the particular field, is often able to reconstruct the course of events and assign the cause or causes of the particular event.

The paradigm of such a research design was developed many years ago in a study sponsored by the United States Department of Commerce (see Table 1).[10]

7. MOTIVATION RESEARCH

The advent of psychoanalysis has tempted social scientists into efforts to supplement reason analysis by devices that try to penetrate at least the upper layers of unconscious motivations by means of tests designed to reveal personality characteristics or specific unconscious attitudes. Again, its tool is the interview, but its aim is not reconstruction of a more or less conscious decision but the discovery of layers of subconscious motivations. The direct question *why* fails here, because the respondent himself, by definition, does not know his reasons, even if accorded all the patience

[9] For examples, see H. Kalven, Jr., and H. Zeisel, *The American Jury* (Boston: Little, Brown, 1966), under "Confrontation of Methods" in the Index.

[10] This is a slightly modified and simplified version of a table reproduced in H.R. Doc. No. 462, 75th Cong., 3d Sess. 11 (1938). Unfortunately, this study was not based on a representative sample, nor was the mechanical examination of the cars sufficiently thorough. A variant of this method was used in the study designed to find out what reasons led to the occasional disagreement between jury and the presiding judge in jury trials. Here, the judge was the expert who made the assessment, often of course after having discussed the matter with the jury. See Kalven and Zeisel, *The American Jury, op. cit.*, especially Chapter 7, "The Logic of Explanation."

TABLE 1
Analysis of Immediate Causes of 30 Accidents

		%
Driver violations		
Excessive speed	20	
Improper turns	10	
Improper passing and others	5	
Total		35
Driver errors		41
Car defects		5
Road properties		11
Miscellaneous		8
Total		100%

and help of a good interviewer. This approach has acquired the label *motivation research.*

Sometimes the approach is limited to or aided by standardized tests, such as the Minnesota Multiphase Personality Inventory or the Rorschach test. More often it is a test developed for the specific purpose, asking the interviewee to answer a set of attitude questions or to draw a picture, as best he can, of a designated object, such as an automobile, a house, a man, or the like. To be useful, all such efforts must be predicated on the analyst's ability to establish a meaningful connection between the revealed attitudes and the behavior that is to be explained.[11]

8. THE INDIRECT EXPERIMENT

I shall now turn to a type of experiment that has developed in response to many obstacles that hamper directly controlled experimentation with human beings or social institutions. Let me begin by telling you of an experiment that was conducted in my narrower sphere of interest, in the area of legal procedure. Most civil suits in our courts go through a procedure called pre-trial in which the judge confers with the litigants to find out whether the case can be settled or, if not, prepared for trial so that it can proceed economically. Although a great many cases are settled at these pre-trials, the suspicion was advanced that the cases would have been settled anyway and that pre-trying cases might waste time that in our overcrowded courts could be better devoted to trying cases.

[11] As to the theory, see Paul F. Lazarsfeld, "Progress and Fad in Motivation Research," Proceedings of the Third Annual Seminar on Social Science for Industry Motivation, Stanford Research Institute, 1955, pp. 11–23. As to the praxis, see Herta Herzog's classic, in Herzog and Gaudet, *The Invasion from Mars—a Study in the Psychology of Panic* (Princeton, N.J.: Princeton University Press, 1940). See also, Ernest Dichter, *Handbook of Consumer Motivation* (New York: McGraw-Hill, 1964); James V. McNeal (ed.), *Dimensions of Consumer Behavior* (New York: Appleton-Century-Crofts); Joseph Newman (ed.), *Unknowing the Consumer* (New York: John Wiley & Sons, 1966); and Karen A. Machover, *Personality Projection in the Drawing of the Human Figure* (Springfield, Ill.: C. C. Thomas, 1949).

A simple experiment could have been designed to test this hypothesis: simply pre-try a random half of the cases, do not pre-try the other half, and see whether the proportion of settled cases is higher in the one group than in the other. The difficulty was that the courts thought they could not rightfully exclude any litigant from pre-trial arbitrarily as long as some litigants were granted this right. In this situation, the following compromise solution was developed: the cases were randomly divided into two groups; all cases in the one group were called for pre-trial; the cases in the other group were pre-tried only if one or both litigants requested it. The redesigned experiment, then, compared obligatory pre-trial with optional pre-trial, hence allows no direct assessment of pre-trial as such. Moreover, the design would have come to naught if all litigants had requested pre-trial. As it happened, only about half of them did, hence the experiment worked and, incidentally, revealed with great clarity obligatory pre-trial as a complete waste of time. There were just as many settlements in the optional group as among the pre-tried cases, and the trials that evolved in the pre-trial group lasted just as long as the trials of the cases in the optional group.[12] The important thing to note is, that although the decision as to whether a case is to be pre-tried was not made randomly, the experiment was nevertheless a controlled one because the original assignment of cases to the two groups was made at random.

Let me tell you of another indirect experiment in the area of civil procedure. It was suggested that splitting civil trial into two parts, so that damages are litigated only if liability is found, would save much needed trial time. The procedure was tested by assigning cases at random to the judges in a court, but then leaving it to the judge as to whether or not he wanted to apply the procedure. Here the experiment hinged on the hope that judges would apply the rule with differential frequencies, which they did. The procedure, incidentally, revealed itself as an effective means of curtailing trial time.[13]

We might speculate here for a moment on how—what I have called here—the indirect experiment might be used to resolve, for instance, the smoking-cancer controversy. It hinges, as you know, on the lack of final experimental proof, since one cannot very well order one random group of people to smoke and order another not to smoke. But there is something close to it that one could do. Suppose we formed, by randomization, two interchangeable groups of smokers. We then try to persuade the one group to reduce or desist from smoking. It does not matter how we attempt this—by persuasion, threat, or even by bribery. What matters alone is that we succeed to some extent. Any subsequent difference in cancer mortality between the two groups could then be ascribed with considerable certainty to the reduction in smoking.

---

[12] M. Rosenberg, *The Pretrial Conference and Effective Justice* (New York: Columbia University Press, 1964).

[13] H. Zeisel and T. Callahan, "Split Trials and Time Saving: A Statistical Analysis," *Harvard Law Review*, Vol. 76 (1963), pp. 1606–1625.

9. DEVIATION FROM PREDICTION

Still another device for circumventing the obstacles of experimentation must be mentioned. To be sure, it is but a special case of refining retrospective cross-tabulations, but it has important features of its own. The British Home Office, for example, was eager to learn whether certain methods of parole supervision of ex-convicts would reduce the rate of recidivism. Since it seemed inopportune or impossible to make a controlled experiment of it, the following method was used. There is considerable knowledge from prior studies on the differential rates of parole success for different types of ex-convicts. Thus it was found that family ties, work habits, extent of criminal record, and other factors, in combination, were good predictors of the differential success rate. The rationale of the parole supervision study utilized this prediction by comparing, not the crude success rate in the experimental and control group, but rather the *deviation* of the crude success rate from the rate predicted for these individuals by the prediction formula. The difference between the predicted and the actual (crude) success rate was then ascribed to the treatment.

10. THE PANEL

There is one last device that deserves mention in this context—the panel operation. Not that it does not constitute by itself a special mode of causal analysis. Rather, its usefulness may be compared to that of a ladder that facilitates orderly access to data. Its essence is that it allows us several observations of the same unit—of a person, a family, or what not—over time. Its major methodological advantage is that it enables us to learn the sequence of events and, thereby, to learn to distinguish between cause and effect, since the one must precede the other in time. In addition, the panel has the advantage of allowing us to collect much more information about any one unit than the one-shot survey can provide. The panel can thus be used retrospectively as a means of providing more and more orderly survey data, but it can also be used as a vehicle for controlled experimentation.

At this point the ring closes, and we arrive where we had started—at the controlled experiment, which by definition requires at least one "before" and one "after" observation of the experimental and the control unit.

The survey analyst customarily looks at a market with the aim of describing its broadest dimensions. He examines the entire field of a product's distribution, and his first concern is to see what the brand's position is, who the customers are, what is the unexploited sales potential. In short, the analyst is apt to see the market as an aggregate, represented in consumer research by his sample, also an aggregate.

Since the science of statistics has long since demonstrated to everyone's satisfaction that a comparatively small sample can accurately represent the distribution of characteristics in a large population, samples are conventionally selected to provide individual respondents scattered at random throughout the population being measured. Therein, argues Allen Barton, is a fundamental defect.

In real life, he points out, behavior in the market, as in other aspects of social life, is strongly governed by interpersonal relationships which can only be studied in context and never on the basis of the isolated and unrelated responses of single individuals taken one by one. By all indications, personal influence is a strong force in the market place. For this reason, the author argues that market research should make much broader use of sampling innovations which can permit this influence to be detected and accurately described. Professor Barton is Director of the Bureau of Applied Social Research at Columbia University.

10. Personal Influence Revisited*

ALLEN H. BARTON

Random sampling of individuals is a sociological meatgrinder. You can study mice and frogs by putting them through a hamburger machine and looking at every hundredth cell under a microscope, but you tend to lose information about anatomy and physiology that way. Structure and function get lost, and we are left with cell biology.

Why should anyone do something as foolish as sampling at random or taking every *n*th individual? Don't they know that this tears the individual from his social context and positively guarantees never getting anyone who interacts with anyone else in the sample? Don't they know that interaction, mutual perceptions and expectations, communication, and social control go on between people?

The answer is that for certain purposes, random sampling is not so foolish. If we want to describe accurately the individual characteristics of some large population, the sample survey is a miracle of efficiency. Instead of waiting ten years for a few limited pieces of information from the census, we can find out about an incredible range of attitudes, characteristics, and behaviors of the U.S. population by interviewing only a few thousand people. It is small wonder that for the last 30 years social scientists have used sample surveys for all they were worth.

The trouble begins when we want to use them for more than they are worth. When we have data from a large descriptive study on IBM cards, the temptation is to do more than just tabulate them: we cross-tabulate them. And by cross-tabulating, we think we can analyze the causes of the behaviors and attributes we have described or the consequences of exposure to various stimuli which we have measured. And so survey analysis is born, and with it all manner of statistical and sociological sin. For there is an inherent contradiction between the sample design which produces accurate descriptive statistics and the sample design which you need to explain attitudes and behavior, trace the effects of stimuli, or analyze the operation of a social sub-system.

A good descriptive survey is designed to reduce sampling error. In the formula for computing sampling error there are two major variables: the

*Presented to the Market Research Council, May 20, 1966.

total sample size, and the correction for clustering. Clustering of interviews is something which survey researchers do to save money on the field work, by reducing interviewer travel and by making sample selection easier. To reduce the sampling error due to clustering as much as possible, we keep the clusters small and scattered. When it comes to analysis, we pretend they didn't exist. Respondents are identified only by individual characteristics and, at best, region and size of place.

If our aim, on the other hand, is to understand human behavior rather than simply to record it, we want to know about their primary groups, their neighborhoods, their organizational memberships, and their communities; about interaction, communication, role expectations, and social control. We would like family clusters, neighborhood clusters, friendship clusters, work group clusters, community clusters. We would like to put social structure and social process back in. Of course, this often interferes with obtaining accurate descriptive statistics on large populations. There are sometimes ingenious ways of trying to get both good descriptive statistics and good analysis of behavior in context, but the conflict of goals is there and must be recognized.

Over the last 20 years or so, there have been many experiments in survey design which have tried to put social structure back into the picture. Many of these have been carried out by Paul Lazarsfeld and his collaborators at Columbia and by his students who have moved on to do research elsewhere. I would like to report today on some of these devices and their problems. They include:

1. Measurement of *perceived interpersonal environments;*
2. Use of cluster samples to measure *social contexts;* and
3. Use of sociometric samples to measure actual *interpersonal environments.*

I will also discuss some of the social processes which are revealed by these studies. These include *multiplier effects* and *dampening effects.* I will suggest the relevance of these processes to the study of consumer behavior. And finally I will indicate some of the unmet needs for research on these processes and unsolved methodological problems.

1. THE INFLUENCE OF PERCEIVED INTERPERSONAL ENVIRONMENTS

In 1940 Lazarsfeld applied the panel method to the study of voting behavior in order to test hypotheses about the influence of mass media on voting.[1] An ordinary random sample of one county was taken (no effort was made to be representative of the whole country), and respondents were reinterviewed as many as six times in the course of the campaign. This permitted identification of those who changed their voting intention. The changers were asked carefully designed, open-ended questions concerning external

[1] Paul F. Lazarsfeld, Bernard Berelson, and Hazel Gaudet, *The People's Choice* (2nd edition; New York: Columbia University Press, 1948).

stimuli and internal dispositions which led them to behave as they did; the method of *reason analysis* was used. This reason analysis revealed that voters reported much more often that they were influenced by other people in their social environments than by the mass media.

Therefore, the next election panel study designed by Lazarsfeld in 1948 included many questions on which respondents could report the political complexion of their social environment: the party affiliation of their three closest friends, three fellow workers, their family members, and so on. The 1948 study documented the fact that most people move in socially and politically homogeneous groupings; that people whose group memberships are non-homogeneous are more likely to change their minds or withdraw; and that one function of the campaign is to activate the majority norms within such groupings and bring back to conformity individual members who have drifted away during periods when politics was not an object of group attention.

TABLE I
Effect of a Perceived Interpersonal Environment*

	August-to-November voting changes				
	Stayed same party as in August	*Became non-voter*	*Changed to opposite party*	*Total*	*n*
Majority of co-workers:					
Same party as respondent	77%	17%	6%	100%	(192)
Unknown or undecided	65%	24%	11%	100%	(95)
Opposite party	64%	26%	11%	100%	(47)

*Bernard Berelson, Paul F. Lazarsfeld, and William N. McPhee, *Voting* (Chicago: University of Chicago Press, 1954), p. 122.

A typical table of the 1948 election study shows the effects of perceived preferences of fellow workers. Note that most were not exposed to contrary environments (see Table I). Family had considerably stronger effects than co-workers; while friends were a relatively weak influence.

The difficulties of using respondent reports of their social context are obvious: they may not accurately perceive it, or they may not be conscious of characteristics of the context which in fact influence them. To be sure, what men perceive to be real can influence them; but that does not mean the reality is irrelevant. Ideally we would like to know both.

2. THE USE OF CLUSTER SAMPLES TO MEASURE SOCIAL CONTEXTS

Suppose we want to know what the individual's social context is really like—how do we measure it? The problem is relatively easy when we deal with easily identifiable organizational units, like workshops, offices, and schools. We have good reason to expect that people are in actual contact with the other members of their work group or school class and that these groups are important to them. Over the last ten years we have used "contextual samples" in the study of printers' participation in their union, of college professors' reactions to McCarthyism, of lawyers' ethical behavior in urban law offices, and of academic dishonesty in college.

Typical measures of "direct context effect" show that individual behavior is about as much influenced by the frequency of a given attitude in the context as by the individual's own predispositions. An example can be drawn from the study of student dishonesty. We took clusters averaging 55 students from 99 colleges; the "climate of disapproval" for each college was measured by the proportion of the sample at that college who disapproved strongly of several specific practices (see Table II).

TABLE II

Effect of Social Context on Behavior, Controlling Past Behavior of Individual*

	Percentage ever cheating in college	
	Among those who did cheat in high school	*Among those who did not cheat in high school*
Climate of disapproval of the college:		
Strong	45%	21%
Moderate	64%	34%
Weak	78%	46%

*William Bowers, *Student Dishonesty* (New York: Bureau of Applied Social Research, 1964), p. 158.

The study of lawyers' ethics dealt with much smaller units, i.e., law offices of from 2 to 14 people. A random sample of New York law offices was taken, and everyone in the sample offices was interviewed, thereby producing a clustered random sample of the New York bar complete with law-office contexts. The "office climate" was measured by the proportion of members who supported a strict versus a permissive orientation to the canons of ethics. Results were similar to the student dishonesty findings: when the individual lawyer's predispositions were held constant, the office climate had a major effect on ethical behavior. This effect could be specified as occurring most strongly in offices that were highly sociable and on members who had been in the office for a longer period of time. It was almost non-existent for short-time members of unsociable offices (see Table III).

Application of contextual sampling outside of formal organizations is more difficult, since it is not so clear how to delimit relevant contexts. A study of attitudes toward fallout shelters interviewed clusters centered on families which had built a shelter, sampling neighbors at various distances. In this case the object was not to study the effect of the group on the individual's behavior, but the effect of the individual's behavior on the group. It is fair to say that the impact of shelter-building was rather slight, but it

TABLE III
Effect of Social Context on Behavior, Varying Length and Intensity of Exposure*

	Percentage violating ethical standards of bar					
	Lawyers less than 5 years in the office			*Lawyers 5 years or more in the office*		
	Office sociability			*Office sociability*		
	Low	*Medium*	*High*	*Low*	*Medium*	*High*
Office climate:						
Permissive	24%	42%	48%	36%	38%	62%
Strict	21%	19%	26%	19%	9%	4%
	+ 3	+23	+22	+17	+29	+58

*Jerome E. Carlin, *Lawyers' Ethics* (New York: Russell Sage Foundation, 1966), p. 100.

is noticeable that the near neighbors seem to have a "sour grapes" attitude (see Tabie IV).

We have few other examples of contextual studies using locality clusters. An unusual one involved the experimental creation of different contexts. A campaign for birth control in Formosa compared three areas: those in which half of the households received both a mailing and a visit (with the remainder divided equally between mail only and nothing), those in which one-third received the combined mailing and visit, and those where only one-fifth were given intensive treatment. The percentage of women who responded varied both with individual treatment and the density of treatment in their area (see Table V). The "spillover effect" on those not directly contacted was only slightly greater where coverage was dense. However, the effect of being in a denser context on those who were visited was considerable.

A table from Lipset, Trow, and Coleman's *Union Democracy* shows one of the limitations of contextual analysis. Printers from many different

TABLE IV

Effect of Having a Fallout Shelter Owner on the Same Block*

	*Shelter owners***	*Neighbors on same block*	*More distant neighbors*	*Effect of being on same block as shelter*
Attitudes toward shelters:				
Favor fallout shelters	91%	51%	57%	−6
Favor spending local tax money on community shelters	67%	49%	58%	−9
Believe a person has an even chance or better of surviving atomic war if in a shelter	90%	65%	74%	−9
Relations to neighbors:				
People in neighborhood would help each other in event of attack	72%	64%	70%	−6
Visit three or more of ten nearest neighbors	72%	63%	60%	+3
Attitudes toward war:				
There will always be war	51%	53%	59%	−6
A test ban won't work	61%	64%	60%	+4

*Gene N. Levine and John Modell, *The Threat of War and American Public Opinion* (New York: Bureau of Applied Social Research, unpublished report, 1964).
**Differences between shelter owners and non-owners are probably due to prior factors which make some people build shelters and are not effects of shelter ownership. Such "self-selection" does not apply to the neighbors of fallout shelter owners.

shops were sampled. The degree of consensus of the shop was computed using voting statistics from union elections. In small shops there was a clear relationship between consensus and participation, but in large shops the degree of consensus of the shop context had no effect (see Table VI).

Lipset explains that in large shops,

> the more voluntary networks of on-the-job social relations (can) segregate into politically homogeneous cliques, and thus not be endangered by political involvements of their members, while the shop as a whole divides politically.

In other words, the shop ceases to be the effective social context of the individual printer, at least in some respects, when it gets so large that homogeneous cliques can develop within it. To obtain information on the in-

TABLE V

Effects of an Experimentally Created Context*

	Percentage of married women, aged 20 to 39, accepting birth control			
	1/2 house-holds visited	*1/3 house-holds visited*	*1/5 house-holds visited*	*Effect of denser coverage*
Individual was:				
Visited	17%	12%	12%	+5
Mail only	7%	5%	6%	+1
Not contacted	7%	5%	5%	+2
Direct effect of visit	+10	+ 7	+ 6	
Direct effect of mail	0	0	+ 1	
Indirect effect on those not contacted	+ 7	+ 5	+ 5	

*Bernard Berelson and Ronald Freedman, "A Study in Fertility Control," *Scientific American,* Vol. 210 (May, 1964), p. 34.

TABLE VI

Effect of a Contextual Variable, Conditioned by Size of Unit*

	Percentage of men active in union politics	
	Large shops (over 30)	*Small shops (under 30)*
High consensus (more than 63% vote for majority party in shop)	43% (105)	29% (125)
Low consensus (less than 63% vote for majority party in shop)	43% (160)	7% (125)
Shop context effect	0	+22

*S. M. Lipset, M. A. Trow, and J. S. Coleman, *Union Democracy* (Glencoe, Illinois: The Free Press, 1956), p. 167.

TABLE VII
Conformity to Context Related to Friendship Patterns*

	Percentage having best friend in same shop (among men in small shops)	
	Men high in ideological sensitivity	*Men low in ideological sensitivity*
Conformists in high-consensus shops	48% (31)	48% (60)
All men in low-consensus shops	34% (12)	42% (19)
Nonconformists in high-consensus shops	22% (18)	48% (25)

*S. M. Lipset, M. A. Trow, and J. S. Coleman, *Union Democracy* (Glencoe, Illinois: The Free Press, 1956), p. 169.

dividual's effective contexts within the shop, Lipset falls back on questions by which respondents characterize their perceived interpersonal environment. He asks respondents whether they know personally any active members of the two union parties. The proportion who know active members of both parties—thus having a heterogeneous interpersonal environment—is very low in small shops, rises in middle-sized shops, but falls off again in the large shops. He also asks respondents whether their best printer friends work in their own shop or elsewhere. Those few printers in small, high-consensus shops who have "nonconformist" politics and who are concerned with ideology are less likely to have their closest friends within the shop (see Table VII).

3. THE USE OF SOCIOMETRIC SAMPLES TO MEASURE INTERPERSONAL ENVIRONMENTS

Ideally we would like to know both the actual and the perceived interpersonal environments. An approach to this was made in a pilot study of attitudes, perceptions, and behavior relating to racial integration in housing, by Kenneth Lenihan.[2] For years survey researchers have been asking people whether they would object if a Negro family of the same economic level as other people on the block moved into their block; there has been a slow decrease in objections over the years, but housing remains one of the major

[2] Kenneth Lenihan, "Attitudes toward Negroes in a New Jersey Suburb," unpublished report, Bureau of Applied Social Research, 1964.

forms of discrimination outside the South. Lenihan asked a sample of respondents this question, and also asked them whether they thought their next door neighbor would object. Then he interviewed the neighbor, asking the same questions. The result was a sample of pairs. Of the 31 pairs on which information was fully available, 12 consisted of two people who said they would not object. In *no* case did both members of the pair accurately perceive the other's lack of objection, and in 9 cases each misperceived the other.

That misperception of the interpersonal environment has consequences is suggested by the fact that those who saw their neighbors as objecting to a Negro moving in were less likely to be willing to sell their house to a Negro, even when they themselves had no objection to a Negro on the block.

The most elaborate study of effects of interpersonal environments is Walter Wallace's *Student Culture*. Freshmen at a small, midwestern college were studied using the panel method, in September, November, and April of their first year. In November and April they were also asked to go through a list of the student body. Each freshman checked off the names of the other students he recognized, indicating how many hours a week he spent with each, and whether he liked or disliked him. The rest of the student body was surveyed just once, in November, since the study was limited to influences on freshmen's attitudes and behavior and not of freshmen's influences on the others. Thus, we have a sociometric panel study, in which change in individual respondents can be related to the characteristics of their interpersonal environments.

Such relationships were indeed found. One attitude which changed a good deal during the first year was the importance which students placed on getting high grades. There was a sharp fall in the proportion who rated high grades as important during the first two months, bringing freshmen into closer agreement with upperclassmen (see Table VIII).

This shift was inhibited by having an interpersonal environment composed mainly of freshmen of one's own sex; it was encouraged by having

TABLE VIII

Overall Change by New Members Toward Old-Member Norms*

	Percentage with high-grades orientation			
	September	*November*	*Actual change possible*	*n*
Freshman men	78%	50%	.35	(129)
Freshman women	73%	35%	.52	(148)
Nonfreshman men		42%		(293)
Nonfreshman women		27%		(240)

*Walter A. Wallace, *Student Culture* (Chicago: Aldine Publishing Co., 1966), p. 51.

TABLE IX
Effects of Social Composition of the Interpersonal Environment*

	Percentage with high-grades orientation			
	September	*November*	*Actual change / possible*	*n*
Freshman men				
Proportion of freshman men in IE				
High	77%	58%	–.25	(65)
Low	75%	37%	–.51	(59)
Proportion of freshman women in IE				
High	75%	48%	–.36	(65)
Low	76%	49%	–.36	(59)
Proportion of nonfreshman men in IE				
High	76%	39%	–.49	(59)
Low	75%	57%	–.24	(65)
Proportion of nonfreshman women in IE				
High	78%	46%	–.41	(63)
Low	74%	51%	–.31	(61)
Freshman women				
Proportion of freshman men in IE				
High	72%	34%	–.53	(71)
Low	74%	35%	–.53	(74)
Proportion of freshman women in IE				
High	79%	44%	–.44	(72)
Low	67%	25%	–.63	(73)
Proportion of nonfreshman men in IE				
High	65%	29%	–.55	(75)
Low	81%	40%	–.51	(70)
Proportion of nonfreshman women in IE				
High	72%	29%	–.60	(76)
Low	74%	41%	–.45	(69)

*Walter A. Wallace, *Student Culture* (Chicago: Aldine Publishing Co., 1966), p. 52.

many upperclassmen of one's own sex in the interpersonal environment. Cross-sex relationships seem to have little influence (see Table IX). Change was also related to the specific attitudes of the upperclassmen with whom the freshman was in contact (see Table X).

The impact of the various segments of the interpersonal environment varied with the topic and with the phase of the student's socialization. Many results of the analysis were complicated and even inconsistent. But the power of "interpersonal environment analysis" in studying attitude change is clear from these examples. It could be especially valuable in analyzing mass shifts in which each individual plays two roles, that of

TABLE X

Effects of the Attitude Distributions of the Interpersonal Environment*

	Percentage with high-grades orientation			
	September	*November*	*Actual change / possible*	*n*
Freshman men				
Nonfreshman men in IE are:				
Above average in grades orientation	82%	62%	–.24	(39)
Below average in grades orientation	73%	42%	–.42	(84)
Nonfreshman women in IE are:				
Above average in grades orientation	71%	53%	–.25	(34)
Below average in grades orientation	78%	44%	–.44	(82)
Freshman women				
Nonfreshman men in IE are:				
Above average in grades orientation	77%	43%	–.44	(40)
Below average in grades orientation	72%	32%	–.56	(107)
Nonfreshman women in IE are:				
Above average in grades orientation	79%	62%	–.22	(29)
Below average in grades orientation	72%	28%	–.61	(118)

*Walter A. Wallace, *Student Culture* (Chicago: Aldine Publishing Co., 1966), p. 56.

the influencer and the influenced, and in which a crucial question is whether a new attitude or behavior will be damped by the weight of the conservative environment, or will spread until it becomes the new majority pattern, multiplying its effects as it goes.

4. SNOWBALLS, MULTIPLIERS, AND DAMPENERS

The measurement of interpersonal environments is fairly easy when we deal with a community of 1000 or less, as in the college study or certain studies of small rural communities. It simply requires interviewing everybody and asking some sociometric questions on contacts. In a very large population of hundreds of thousands or millions, we obviously cannot interview everybody. Are we then to be restricted to inquiring about their perceived interpersonal environments?

Here is where the original *Personal Influence*[3] study attempted an innovation: the snowball sample. A randomly selected panel was interviewed and reinterviewed in a large community. Changers were asked to reconstruct the processes which led to their decisions. When particular people were mentioned as an influence, they were to be followed up and interviewed. Characteristics of leader-follower pairs could be studied, the influencers compared with the influenced, and the "influence structure" of the community described. There were serious technical difficulties in the follow-up interviews, and a good deal of the analysis had to be based on self-reported "opinion leadership" within the original sample rather than on the follow-up of influence as reported by the person affected.

This technique of over 20 years ago has never been adequately developed to study interpersonal environments in large populations. One need not undertake the difficult task of following up reported influencers with respect to a particular decision; one could instead follow up the three or four or five people with whom the respondent reports he is in most frequent contact—his best friends, his most frequently seen relatives, his closest co-workers, his neighbors with whom he talks most often.

Such a design was proposed for a study (never executed) designed to assess the impact of a major community action program in Harlem. We planned to take a basic sample of 500 households, interviewing male and female heads where present. Then we would ask each for names and addresses of the friends, relatives, and neighbors with whom they talked most frequently and to whom they felt closest, and we would "snowball out" to interview three of them who lived within the city. Both the basic sample of perhaps 800 people in 500 households, and the "snowball sample" of around 2400 friends, relatives, and neighbors, would be reinterviewed every half year during the operation of a massive program of help to the people of the ghetto. The program might bring direct benefits of jobs, educational

[3] Elihu Katz and Paul F. Lazarsfeld, *Personal Influence* (Glencoe, Illinois: The Free Press, 1955).

improvement, housing, or community organization participation to members either of the basic sample or the snowball sample. For each cluster of people linked by sociometric ties, we would examine whether participation in the action program by one member tended to "multiply" by raising the aspirations of and activating *other members* of the cluster, as well as the one directly involved; or whether it tended to be "dampened" by the discouragement or cynicism of the friends, relatives, and neighbors of the individual who was directly reached by the program, preventing him from changing and preventing others from being influenced. Would we find "chain reactions," or a massive "locking in" of people by their interpersonal environments? Under what conditions does one or the other mechanism operate?

We believe that it is impossible to understand why some campaigns to influence people succeed, and others fail, unless one looks at these mechanisms. We know a good deal about their operation in presidential elections. We know a little about how they operate in disseminating information among professionals, from the studies by Coleman, Katz, and Menzel. But they are seldom studied in "evaluation research," even though by now we know that most campaigns to educate and influence people fail.

A basic reason for not using the snowball design is its cost. To study the interpersonal environments of 800 people in a small, closed community, we just need to interview the 800 and include sociometric questions. To study the interpersonal environments of 800 people in a large community, we need to interview at least 2400 additional people, who are not a representative sample because they are chosen by basic sample respondents, and therefore are of little use for describing the total population. They are only useful for explaining what happens in interactions with the first 800 people. But for that, they may be indispensable. It is a question of what one wants—a good description based on 3200 interviews, or a good analysis of what determines people's behavior based on 800 people studied in their interpersonal environments. It would obviously be worth experimenting with inexpensive means of obtaining selected information from the "snowball" part of the sample, perhaps by use of telephone interviews or mailed questionnaires.

The relation of these themes to consumer research should be obvious, even though not one of the examples has dealt specifically with decisions to buy goods (unless a fallout shelter counts as a good). Social networks are involved in three basic processes influencing buying:

1. Communication of information about products, especially new ones;
2. Enforcement of social norms, which regulate certain consumption behavior which is considered appropriate or inappropriate, required or condemned, prestigeful or in bad taste, in given social circles; and
3. Linking certain behavior to participation in group life, as where certain games or leisure activities become the requirement for sociability, whether it be bowling, golf, drinking at the pub, gardening, or

travelling far from home so that one can talk about it with one's neighbors.

The information, norms, and fashions communicated within these networks are only partially influenced by deliberate efforts of advertising or public relations campaigns; they also reflect personal experience with products and with corporations, and underlying cultural values in which people are socialized in primary group relationships. To understand the complex and recalcitrant behavior of man in the market place, we must understand not only his motivations, but also his social structure.

In understanding social structures and their influence on social processes, we need basic research and experimentation with new methods capable of putting social structure back into survey research. We need to know much more about the kinds of interpersonal contacts which city-people have and how they are influenced by them; we need to try out different means of clustering and snowballing to find workable sample designs which still preserve some of the anatomy of social life. Just because hamburger is cheap, we should not have to put everything through the meatgrinder.

The chief purpose of marketing research is commonly considered to be that it permits a manufacturer to sell his product more efficiently by understanding both his customers and those of his competitors. In this view the company is the actor, playing on the susceptibilities of passive consumers.

The next paper suggests that market research is really an important part of a feedback process through which manufacturers can become more responsive to the opportunities which result from differences in wants and motivations among a complex public. Nelson Foote suggests that the consumer is served by the corporate practice of segmenting the market into components which differ in their characteristic tastes. This practice, he believes, enhances the likelihood that companies will establish real differences in the products they sell rather than merely accentuate imaginary differences in brand images or advertising themes.

To the extent that research can lead to segmentation, it also makes for a more vivid competition with respect to the values represented by competing brands of merchandise. Dr. Foote, formerly professor of sociology at Cornell University and at the University of Chicago, is consultant in the marketing and public relations services division of the General Electric Company.

11. Market Segmentation as a Competitive Strategy*

NELSON N. FOOTE

Let us assume we have made the discovery that consumers of ice cream differ significantly in their preferences for chocolate, strawberry, and vanilla. And let us assume that these flavor preferences are not distributed randomly among all kinds of people, but are differentially associated with some other characteristic of customers for ice cream, such as hair color, and that these associations are substantial in degree and practical to ascertain. For example, let us say that brunettes tend strongly to like chocolate, redheads to favor strawberry, and blondes, vanilla. Finally, let us imagine that this pattern is just that simple and orderly—product differences nicely match customer differences.

Then what?

What is the businessman who wants to sell ice cream in this market to do about our findings? Is he to conclude that he should offer all three flavors, the same as the rest of the industry, lest he forego any important source of sales? Or should he try to serve only blondes and brunettes, since there are not enough redheads to make serving them profitable? Or should he seek to establish a reputation as the producer of the finest Dutch chocolate ice cream, so that he captures nearly all that segment of the market? Or should he go after the great mass of vanilla fans, by upgrading this lowly flavor with a French accent? Or should he take account of his newness or smallness in the industry and challenge the incumbent giants of the trade by introducing pistachio or frozen custard? Or should he offer the normal product line of his industry, but allow some major chain of retail outlets to apply its store brand to his product? Should he go after the door-to-door trade with a very short line—like Neapolitan only—or open his own chain of soda fountains with 28 flavors? Or should he be creative and try to think up some utterly new way to exploit his knowledge of differing customer preferences, since all these strategies—and more besides—are already in use today in the ice cream business?

Plainly, even if one knew far more than is known already about patterns

*Presented to the Consumer Market Segmentation Conference, American Marketing Association, Chicago, February 24, 1967.

of correlation between product and customer differences in any particular market, it takes a lot of thinking and doing before this knowledge can be turned into a calculated competitive strategy. Meanwhile we find examples of marketing managers who have very successfully employed a strategy of market segmentation, quite without the resources of detailed information that as professional marketers we like to think are indispensable to decision-making in matters of such complexity and risk.

It seems important throughout discussion of market segmentation to recognize that the main source of interest in the concept is its potential value as a competitive strategy. There may be quite a number of people whose interest is in promoting the sale or purchase of data regarding the "stratigraphics" of consumer choice. But unless these data can be put to practical use in improving or defending the market position or profits of their user, only the data seller will benefit, and he not for long. So my self-chosen assignment here is to bear down on the task of thinking out the use of such data in actual marketing management. Although I make my living as a marketing researcher, I think that we need more thinking on this matter as much as we need more research.

Immediately, however, the question arises of who is going to discuss competitive strategy in public—especially in the presence of competitors of his own firm—save in empty generalities. A salesman of research data, or representatives of advertising agencies or media, might set forth some hypothetical tactics of market segmentation as a means of soliciting business. But other than personal vanity or the desire to solicit another job, what would induce someone connected with a manufacturer or a retailer to disclose his thinking about competitive strategy? The incentives of professional exchange of technique or the teaching of younger members of the fraternity are not sufficient justification. Many kinds of professional know-how are properly kept proprietary by the firm which paid for their development. If market segmentation is to be analyzed publicly and candidly from the standpoint of an actual competitor in a market, it has to be justified by some benefit that it will bring to this competitor. If it were not my conviction that in fact it is to the benefit of every competing firm that market segmentation be discussed publicly in terms of its implications for competitive strategy, you would not be listening to these words at this moment.

Moreover, we can go one step further and declare that market segmentation as a competitive strategy is also in the interests of customers. If it were not—if it did not offer customers a firmer base for choice among competing offerings and a wider array of genuine choices—it would not work as a competitive strategy. Like any deal, market segmentation is good business only when both parties to the transaction benefit. Market segmentation is thus in effect a logical extension of the basic principles of marketing.

The process of market segmentation, however, when approached as a task of formulating and executing a marketing strategy, involves matching not merely customer characteristics and product characteristics, but a tripartite matching of customers and offerings *and* the array of competitors in the market, as seen from the standpoint of any one competitor within this constellation. If we think of offerings by competitors as expressions of their differing *capabilities*, it will not only be easy to remember the three C's—*customers*, *competitors*, and *capabilities*—but the full task of developing a strategy is more clearly pushed into view.

Let me illustrate concretely by referring to one of our most respected competitors in the Chicago area, the Zenith Radio Corporation. Zenith won a pre-eminent position in the television receiver market some ten years ago by becoming established in the minds of consumers as the leading exemplar of product reliability. Its policy of manufacturing products of good workmanship goes back many years, but during the middle fifties many consumers became quite concerned to identify the set that would, they hoped, give them the least trouble from breakdown. That was when Zenith's market share soared, until it surpassed the erstwhile industry leader. Servicemen and the radio-TV specialty stores with which they are associated lent vigorous aid. Zenith's management and its advertising agency pressed the opportunity that had widened for them. But Zenith had not adopted product reliability as a self-consciously opportunistic, short-term tactic. As far as known, Zenith's strategy was not derived through marketing research, although marketing research by competitors soon verified its efficacy. After some delay, other competitors raised their quality control standards, but none has been able, coming in later on a me-too basis, to emulate Zenith's success. One could quibble about some details of Zenith's reputation—whether hand-wiring is in fact more or less reliable than printed circuits, whether reliability has not been confused to some extent with repairability, whether Zenith sets any longer enjoy the lowest breakdown rate—but from the marketing standpoint, Zenith remains king among that segment of the set market which emphasizes reliability above other virtues when buying sets. The quality standards of the whole industry were forced up by Zenith's success, an outcome of obvious benefit to the consumer, but of at least equal benefit to all the other competitors in the industry, whose personnel devote their whole lives to their industry and much prefer feeling proud of their occupation to feeling ashamed of it.

The meaning of the Zenith example would be very incomplete, however, if we paid attention only to the success story and failed to note that there are many other virtues in television sets which consumers prize besides reliability. If there were not, it would be hard to explain why the Zenith brand share at its zenith rose barely above a fifth of the market. To be sure, Zenith may have preferred its profitability to the greater volume it may have deliberately foregone by upholding a price premium. On the other hand, maybe not; a price premium is just about the loudest advertisement for quality there is.

Meanwhile Zenith's major rival did not simply decide it had to emulate Zenith, but staunchly pursued its strategy of industry statesmanship through the introduction of color, achieving handsome victory and reward from matching its offering with the rising wants of all those customers who were reaching for color in magazines, movies, photography, and other visual media. Alongside these two industry leaders were certain other manufacturers, one of whom has done well by stressing portability and personalization, another by treating the television set as a major piece of furniture, and so on. What is important here is that several competitors held their own or improved their position, even during the period of greatest success by Zenith and RCA, not by seeking to manufacture some hypothetically optimum television set, but by addressing themselves to some substantial segment of the market which *they saw themselves as peculiarly fitted to serve.* The firms which got shaken out during the past dozen years—among which some were big for a time—or which severely lost position can best be described as undistinguishable in their capabilities and offerings, hence undistinguished by consumers.

Now what has been added to the understanding of market segmentation by the example of television receivers? What has been added that is indispensable is the element of competitive capability—a virtue that one particular competitor preeminently possesses—which matches a substantial or rising consumer want. In colloquial terms, what have I got that the other guy hasn't, and which the customer wants badly enough to walk a mile for it?

A few years back, we looked at some commonplace demographic characteristics of television customers arrayed by the brands they tended to favor. When we looked at these demographic characteristics simultaneously, certain results were far more revealing in combination than singly. Only a limited example—because here we are indeed verging on the disclosure of competitive intelligence: we found that one highly meaningful segment of the market—meaningful in terms of sensitivity of discrimination among brands—consisted of households below the median in years of schooling but above the median in income. For convenient reference we called them merely the new-rich, obviously an inexact term. One particular brand seemed to be designed and advertised and priced—properly over-priced, as it were—specifically for this segment, and in fact it enjoyed at that time an inordinate share of their set-buying. Now that company has not noticeably changed its offerings during recent years; they still seem pointed toward the new-rich segment; but its brand share has dwindled substantially. It appears that people with more money than schooling nonetheless are able to learn from experience and do upgrade their taste, given a little time.

The moral of this example is that market segmentation has to be viewed as a continuous process, and marketing strategy has to keep in step with the changing structure of the market. While this implication is probably obvious, perhaps less obvious is the corollary that, just as consumers learn, it is necessary for competitors to learn to exercise differing capabilities from those which may have won them success in the past. And here we come to a matter which lies beyond not only research but also ordinary logic and in the realm of managerial will. Who is to tell a manufacturer that he is capable of doing something he has not done before, and of doing it better than any of his other competitors? By definition, the ordinary kinds of evidence are lacking, because there is no past experience to be projected forward.

In the course of interpersonal relations among individuals, a teacher or a parent may tell a child that he possesses talents he did not previously recognize; the child may then adopt this observation as a conviction about himself which empowers him to demonstrate that it is true. All of us are familiar enough with instances of this outcome not to need to debate whether they occur. The faith of a coach in an athlete, of a critic in a writer, of an employer in an employee, of a wife in a husband, is often the ingredient which brings out a latent capability. Because so little is understood about the process, we cannot make it happen on demand. We are fortunate to recognize it when it does happen, even more so when we spy the opportunity beforehand and do not waste it, for ourselves or for others. Even further beyond present understanding is the possibility of specifying here a reliable formula whereby the management of a company can truly discern those latent talents in its own organization which can be mobilized more effectively by itself than by any of its competitors to satisfy some important emerging customer want.

I do know this, however: recognition of such a talent feeds on itself; it is a cumulative process, a benevolent spiral. I am positive that when the management of Zenith found itself being recognized by consumers for its virtues of good workmanship, it was immensely stimulated to push further in that direction. Thus one of the most valuable functions of marketing research in implementing a strategy of market segmentation is to listen to what is being said about a company by its customers in terms of recognizing its special talents. Developing something that is already there—watering a plant that is already growing, to mix a metaphor—is surely much easier and more likely to succeed than trying to create new capabilities out of whole cloth or, for that matter, borrowing the garments of others, in the sense of imitating or acquiring another company and offering that as an expression of one's own capability.

Part of the growing sophistication of consumers is their increasing interest in the character of the organization they are dealing with. At General Electric we are acutely conscious that certain of our competitors, whose products are no better and sometimes not as good as ours by any measure of product quality, nonetheless enjoy the preference of certain customers. This problem repeatedly confronts the manufacturer who finds himself in competition with retailers who handle only store brands. The whole fascinating issue of what is going to emerge as private branding widens its sway is too vast to open up here. Yet it deserves mention here as constituting market segmentation on an utterly different axis from market segmentation on the axis of product features and brand images.

Segmentation varies in degree as well as in kind. The famous case of the ordinary salt which "rains when it pours" illustrates a valued product feature which has maintained for a particular brand a large and stable market share for many years, while conferring on consumers a valued satisfaction for which they are quite willing to pay a price premium and a rewarding degree of brand loyalty. Many such product features are easily imitated, however, and the reputation for distinctiveness originally achieved may dissolve in the minds of consumers despite advertising. The impermanence of minor product features as a source of competitive distinctiveness and effective market segmentation is a conspicuous failing of the current picture in package goods competition. Like rock-and-roll music, there is too little difference between the new ones and the old ones to make much difference. The proliferation of trivial product differences which appeal to trivial differences among consumers and represent trivial differences among the capabilities of their makers is in effect a mockery of the theory of market segmentation. This proliferation of trivial differences provokes denunciation by producers, retailers, and consumers alike as market fragmentation rather than segmentation and makes an industry vulnerable to the outsider who commences to segment on a different axis. The effective response to the trivialization of market segmentation, however, is not to abandon it as a strategy. To do that would be to abdicate all initiative to competitors. The way out of the expensive waste of trivial segmentation is to engage in serious segmentation, which means segmentation on a larger scale or even on another axis.

Serious, large-scale innovation seems often to come from outside an industry rather than inside. Examples like General Motors in locomotives, Volkswagen in autos, IBM in typewriters, Corning in housewares, Lestoil in detergents, come to mind. Rivalry within a going constellation of competitors seems often to lead to implicit imitation, even when everyone involved is convinced that he is trying to be different from everyone else. How this result occurs is not hard to discern. Close rivals tend very easily to magnify the importance of small differences, whether initiated by themselves or others. If created by another, a close competitor often feels he must come up with a rival innovation but only of corresponding scale.

One detects nothing very distinctive about Silvertone television sets, to mention another respected Chicago competitor. Viewed as manufactured products, they are close to the industry's average line. But where Zenith stresses the reliability built into the product, Sears stresses the services offered by the stores in which Silvertone sets are bought—the promptness of repair service, the easy credit, the ample parking, the special sales well advertised in local newspapers or by direct mail. That is, Sears segments the market on another axis than Zenith. But thus far, Silvertone has encroached far less upon Zenith's clientele than upon the portions of the market occupied by companies whose offerings are less distinctive.

We shall come back to this intriguing question of how far the competition of store brands with manufacturer brands may go before some equilibrium is reached. Some companies as yet have a less urgent private-brand problem anyway, like the auto and gasoline firms and the sellers of services—insurance, banking, air travel, lodging, dry cleaning—which distribute through their own exclusive retail outlets. So for some moments longer, let us stay within the sphere of competition among manufactured products and nationally advertised brands.

Assuming this sphere, we can now state our main hypothesis in further detail: Market segmentation works best as a competitive strategy, i.e., contributes most to the success of competitors and the satisfaction of customers, when product and brand and maker are closely identified in the minds of all concerned.

If we were to assume that one by one more competitors in a market choose to attract particular segments of customers on the basis of correct appraisal of their own special capabilities to satisfy these segments, then the competitors who do not make such deliberate choices will find themselves increasingly confined to the miscellaneous and dwindling residue. As alluded to in our first example, such a development is to some extent a description of what has already happened in some markets, so we may be prophesying simply an intensification of current tendencies rather than anything new under the sun. In other words, self-conscious segmentation may become not only a means of success but the price of survival in a market.

Beyond the ordinary criteria of survival or success as measured in profitability and market share, however, are some other benefits of segmentation to an industry and the various competitors in it. We have mentioned the feeling of pride in their occupation and the quality of its products which most people desire in their life work. Some other benefits of belonging to an industry which steadily adds to the values it offers its customers also deserve explicit recognition. They include the fact that being bested by a competitor whom one respects is easier to accept than being bested by a competitor whom one does not respect. There is a good deal of satisfaction to the producer as well as the consumer in seeing an industry progress over time through advanced applications of science and technology. In an industry plagued with cut-throat price competition instead of value competition, imitation is almost inevitable, because no one can afford the research and development required for innovation. In the vicious downward spiral which obtains in such an industry, jobs are insecure because companies are insecure; and morale and morality seem to decline together. Enough examples spring to mind. An industry trapped in such a spiral, worst of all, has rarely been able to reverse it without outside help, as from major suppliers. DuPont, for example, has struggled quite nobly to raise the plastics molding industry from its swamp. Customers themselves, especially in recent years, have sometimes under these conditions willingly paid substantial premiums for quality and reliability, and this has brought a turnabout, but not before the damage became painful to all concerned.

Both competitors and customers share the benefits of stabilized markets wherein strong degrees of mutual loyalty exist between particular companies and particular segments of customers. Distribution and advertising costs are significantly lower under conditions in which repeat sales make up a high proportion of total sales. The model line of any competitor can be shorter, yet his volume nowadays may be higher, than when he tries to carry everything everyone else in the industry offers. All phases of marketing are much more intelligently, effectively, and efficiently conducted when companies and customers, having chosen each other with care and sophistication, can rely on each other's growing discrimination and sympathetically anticipate the orderly, developmental unfolding and matching of their future wants and capabilities. Some marketing researchers even envision a paradise in which companies will spend as much money in listening as in talking and will make more money doing so.

Let us commence to summarize while injecting a few additional elements into this consideration of market segmentation as a competitive strategy. Our first proposition was that any approach to market segmentation which dealt only with matching customer characteristics with product features was seriously incomplete. The very incentive for exploring market segmentation is to gain advantage—to seek some basis for customer preference—against the array of other competitors and their offerings in a particular market. If one plays only with customer characteristics and product features, he may arrive at the notion of some optimum product for an average customer, in effect, a recipe for reducing his product to commodity status, hence the very opposite of market segmentation, which implies product differentiation. But if he goes to the opposite extreme and tries to equal or surpass the total array of differing products offered by all competitors to all segments of his market, he courts the usual fate of me-too-ism, while suffering impossibly mounting marketing costs. Hence he must seek to identify those offerings which most appeal to some desirable segment of the total market and simultaneously express those capabilities in which he is strongest. The problem of choice here is analogous with that of the boy who must seek distinction from a brother who excels him athletically and another who excels him academically: what talent can he develop which, though different, will seem equivalent in the eyes of those whose approval he seeks? To be all things to all people, to excel in every virtue, is impossible; to be average in all means indistinguishability. Achieving only trivial distinctiveness is a barely-veiled form of imitation, although it can immensely add to promotional expense in an industry. Hence the evolution of a criterion for selecting which customer segments and matching product distinctions to pursue must come from and be disciplined by correct identification of the real strengths and weaknesses of the company itself, as compared with other competitors in its market.

Companies, like individuals, sometimes involuntarily suffer crises of identity, as when merged with other companies. A company embarking upon market segmentation as a competitive strategy is deliberately precipitating a crisis of identity. In place of identity, however, which seems to apply only to the maker of a product rather than to a triple set of interrelations, I believe the concept of theme is more applicable and explanatory of the common element which has to be discovered or invented to match customer characteristic with product feature with company capability. The so-called total marketing approach in its sophisticated form seems finally to come forth with such recognizable themes. The theme of *ease of use* of essentially highly-technical equipment has served Kodak for generations and recurs in numerous notable expressions—from the Brownie to the Instamatic, from the ubiquitous yellow box to the universally recognizable name itself. It illustrates how versatile in its manifestations a theme can be.

But just as product innovation can be trivialized through pointless small variations which make no real contribution to anyone, the concept of theme can be trivialized also, and in fact is, whenever some advertising agency tries to adorn an advertiser with a superficial image that has no real structural relationship to customer segments, competitive constellation, or company capabilities.

The concept of theme is useful in teaching marketing and market segmentation to managers whose experience has been in more exact fields. It helps to avoid the mental blocks that arise when segmentation is grasped as a series of pigeonholes in which various kinds of customers are filed for separate treatment, whereas the manager is eager for all the sales he can get from any source whatever, and finds it hard enough to devise one marketing strategy without having to devise many. To return to our main example, the television receiver market, the theme of reliability can be applied by one manufacturer to all the models in his line and throughout all the functions of marketing in his total marketing program. But the same manufacturer could hardly pursue simultaneously with equal thoroughness and equal success such contrasting themes as modern and traditional cabinetry, portability, technical innovation and retail convenience, although he may keep pace with the industry average in these respects. Market segmentation does not deal with water-tight compartments, but with emphases sufficiently simple and distinctive to win notice and preference among customers to whom they are important, without alienating customers by being deficient in the other virtues which they more or less take for granted.

In terms of demographic and other statistical dimensions by which customers and products may be differentiated, the possibilities for market segmentation are troublesomely infinite. But when the problem of choosing a theme to emphasize is disciplined by attempting to match customers, competitors, and capabilities, these troubles are usually reduced to very few choices that are actually open to a particular firm—though hopefully at least one. The real difficulties of choice are not statistical but spiritual—the anguish of facing up to the fact that if a company is going to move in one direction, it must forego moving in all the others. Such a decision comes especially hard in diversified companies, yet some diversified companies have achieved real synergy through this discipline.

Once this clarifying commitment has been made, its effect on everyone in the organization is to release spontaneous ingenuity in its implementation. A good theme stimulates numberless applications and suggestions, furnishes a guide in numberless subordinate decisions, and eases numberless chores of communication, both inside and outside.

Not only does a positive theme help to mobilize an organization in pursuit of its marketing objectives and heighten their satisfaction, but it wins respect from competitors, even while strengthening and securing its position against them. Spirit is harder to imitate than matter; hardware is easy to copy, but the spirit of a whole organization is not. The competitor who wishes to emulate the success of a competitor's dominant theme must, instead of echoing it, come up with an equivalent theme that uniquely fits himself to his situation, that matches his own three C's.

When my wife was forced to listen to the draft of this paper, her first reaction was that there is much more to marketing than she had previously realized. But there is bound to be more than she or we realize even now. Imagine, for example, how much thicker the atmosphere would get if we tried to push onward into the problems of market segmentation faced by such diversified companies as General Electric which sells many products under mainly a single brand, General Motors which sells mainly one product under several brands, and General Foods which sells many products under many brands, but now seems bent on making the customer aware of the identity of the maker. To add General Mills to this list might also be instructive, if we recall its brief effort to diversify by getting into the electric iron market. There are limits to diversification, at least in consumer markets which are set not only by internal considerations of manageability but externally by the market itself.

We did promise to come back before closing to that matter of competition between the retail sphere and the manufacturing sphere, as an example of market segmentation along radically different axes. It was partly a matter of convenience to set this question aside and partly a matter of conviction. One observes that retailers, regardless of size, seem to want to sell what their customers want to buy. If these customers show no very pronounced preferences among the offerings of various manufacturers, it is probably because there is no very pronounced basis for preference among the competing products. And when this is so, the manufacturers of these more or less indistinguishable commodities are most vulnerable to the substitution of store brands for manufacturer brands. Retailers can compete with retailers in the sale of commodities, by offering store values instead of product values; manufacturers cannot. But when a real basis for product preference exists, the preferred brands either show up on the retailer's shelves, or the retailer is forced to forego substantial business to his competitors who will stock the preferred products. A&P is not about to discontinue Campbell's soup or Heinz ketchup or Jello or other items of this character.

Competition is far from dead among retailers. And as long as competition among retailers exists, manufacturer brands which offer distinctive values to customers will find their way to those customers, if not through one channel, then through another. In a competitive society, the customer will not be denied his choice between less satisfaction and more.

Hence the problem of the manufacturer in confronting the rise of private branding is only in part a task of confronting changes in his environment. The other half of the task is to confront himself and his need for continuous learning and development of his own distinctive capabilities. It is the birthright of the manufacturer to determine the character of his product.

Nowadays we have the phenomenon of the publisher who dreams up an idea for a book and then hires someone to write it. Such offerings by publishers, however, are so poorly received by critics and readers that they have become known as non-books. In the same sense, we might speak of products which no longer portray the identity of their makers as non-products. But the consuming public will always remain more responsive to the author than to the publisher—to the manufacturer than to the middleman—if only the maker will put himself into his product.

Because most market research studies are carried out separately for the competitive advantage of individual clients, they are normally shrouded in secrecy, particularly in the final report stage. This in turn means that a comparison of one study with another is seldom feasible. The lack of comparisons can easily lead to the conclusion that in marketing all cases are unique, all findings are discrete and separate, and few generalizations are possible.

The final paper in this book takes strong issue with this pessimistic point of view. A.S.C. Ehrenberg believes that marketing indeed has laws. He holds that it not only shares the methods of the traditional sciences but that, like those sciences, the findings of marketing research can be expressed precisely in the form of mathematical models which can be tested and checked through fresh research. The author thus echoes some of the conclusion of Hans Zeisel's paper regarding the importance of the controlled experiment. Mr. Ehrenberg, a statistician who has been chairman of the Market Research Society in Great Britain, heads his own research firm, Aske Research Limited, London and New York.

12. Laws in Marketing*

A. S. C. EHRENBERG

One of the commonest beliefs about marketing is that it is much more complex and variable than natural science. Physics and chemistry deal with simple, well-behaved, and highly regular phenomena. Their study easily yields the absolute and invariant laws of science with which we are all so familiar. In contrast, marketing is thought to be far more complex to study. There are more factors at work. It involves intangibles, human beings, and so on. Nothing is constant. Everything varies. There may never be any stable scientific laws in marketing.

Such comments on the difficulties, the complexities, and the instability of marketing processes are only too familiar, both in public and in private. One or two specific references here may suffice. One is to the eight or nine talks by C. West Churchman, Kuhn, Kuehn, Green, Starr, Sebastian Littauer and others given at the Market Research Council in the 1961–1962 season, edited since by Peter Langhoff (1965) and published under the title *Models, Measurement and Marketing*. The special complexities and instabilities of marketing problems are emphasised, together with the probabilistic rhetoric with which we are nowadays supposed to grapple with such problems.

The popular view of marketing complexity was also summarised by Professor Charles K. Ramond, as quoted by Buzzell (1963) in the *Harvard Business Review*: "Variables affecting human behavior interact to such an extent that the familiar 'other-things-being-equal' assumption can lead to mistaken conclusions. Further, physical scientists have generally been able to represent real systems by relatively simple models which can readily be manipulated. But such simple models have not been found adequate to describe human behaviour. And finally, while relationships among physical phenomena are characteristically *stable* over extended time-periods, marketing is thought to be highly *dynamic*. Thus, relationships which seem to describe a system at one time may not hold at some future time."

Personally, I have found nothing in all this talk of special complexities and of new methods which resembles either the known facts of marketing or any successful scientific work that I have come across, whether it was

---

*Presented to the Market Research Council, April 15, 1966, and based on work being carried out for Research Bureau Limited (Unilever).

work for establishing generalised knowledge in the first place or work on then applying such knowledge to practical problems. But I do not here want to criticise the detailed past, except by broadly attempting to demonstrate that there is nothing special about studying marketing (or social science topics generally): ordinary and simple law-like relationships can and do exist, and they can be established by old-fashioned and simple methods of data-handling, such as discovering that variable y varies with variable x under such-and-such a range of empirical conditions, or that so-and-so is a constant.

Laws can be of two broad kinds. There are the scientific generalisations which are directly derived from empirical data, and which for convenience are usually put in a quantitative form. And there are the generalised twaddle kind of laws which are based on insight and armchair experience. Both kinds of law have their uses.

Taking first the twaddle type of law, Ramond (1965) gave us several in a recent Editorial in the *Journal of Advertising Research*. For example:

> *Smith's Law:* "If it's worth doing at all, it's worth doing twice."
> *McAllister's Law:* "If you talk long enough, you will say something intelligent," with its frightful corollary:
> *Corollary:* "If you talk long enough, you will say something stupid."

A further armchair or twaddle law to enunciate now is the fundamental law of science, as follows:

> *The Fundamental Law of Science:* "In general, nothing changes."
> *Corollary:* "A lot of factors *might* affect what one observes, but in practice they don't seem to."

This law has the double advantage of greatly simplifying one's problems and of being true to the facts. If one studies the things which are regular, one will find regularities. Science is as simple as that. All one has to do is to pick on some regular things to study.

This law obviously applies also to marketing. Take any product or brand. Lots of things may vary. But its sales will—IN GENERAL—be pretty much the same as last year. So will the brand's market share and its advertising appropriation and its distribution channels and consumer attitudes and the segmentation of its market. So will the problems of producing the product and of marketing it profitably. Take any sequence of successive market research reports, and all the figures will also be the same from one report to the next: any figure which looks different and therefore interesting is usually wrong—a coding or computing error.

There may be a lot of "intangible" factors in the situation as well, but they only remain intangible because of the fundamental law's corollary, i.e., because they do not seem to have affected the situation anyway. Thus some of the advertising may have changed, and also the price and the package, and the weather is different too. But sales are pretty much the same as they were and so these variable factors just did not matter.

The remarkable thing about the fundamental law that in science nothing changes is that it holds not only for "complex" subjects like marketing where our knowledge is as yet very simple, but also in "simple" fields like physics and chemistry where so much is already known that it all becomes highly complex.

Open a textbook on physics to learn about Factor X and it is very complicated: Factor X is known to vary approximately with so-and-so and so-and-so in such-and-such a manner, as long as variables A and B are controlled and C is negligible, and given that this and that adjustment has been made and all the standard corrections for so-and-so are applied. Outside this limited range of conditions nothing general and systematic is known about Factor X at all. Mr. L's long series of pre-war results on Factor X have been contradicted by 375 experiments carried out under diverse conditions by Professors P, Q, R, and S since. Dr. Z has thoughtfully suggested that differences in the conditions of observation might have been relevant, but his actual results go in the wrong direction and are internally inconsistent, as well as being discrepant with some French and German findings in 1864 and 1897–98 respectively.

In contrast, open a textbook on economics, on management, on marketing, and it is all very simple: there is nothing there. There is not even any empirical evidence of all these *discrepancies* which are always said to exist, of all this alleged change and variance! When people state that something in marketing is not or cannot be constant, what they really mean is that they have hardly observed or measured it at all, and almost certainly not more than once!

Yet irrespective of the state of development of one's subject-matter—whether it is physics or marketing—by studying the things which ARE regular, we come up with regularities: Factor X is systematically related to so-and-so under such-and-such conditions. Last year's brand-leader is still brand-leader.

One very real difficulty does arise in establishing scientific laws (i.e., laws with a full empirical content). It is that people tend to overrate the status of any such law, especially in the natural sciences. Thus, they will think of the older and simpler type of physical law either as an almost self-evident universal statement or as deriving its validity from some background of "theory," instead of its being simply a description of empirical regularities laboriously isolated under a limited range of specified conditions of observation, which are equally known NOT to occur under certain other conditions of observation.

Take for example Boyle's Law in physics. This is that the Pressure P of a body of gas goes up as its Volume V goes down, and vice-versa, i.e., that $P=k/V$, where k is some constant. This approximate relationship has been found to hold for different gases, for different amounts of gas, for different containers, different kinds of apparatus and different experimentors. It is what has been found to hold when the pressure goes up and when the pressure goes down, and when the pressure goes up fast and when it does so slowly, and so on. Equally, however, it has been found that pressure does NOT vary as k/V when the temperature changes, when there is a chemical reaction, when there is a leak in the apparatus, when there is physical absorption or condensation of the gas, or when we tried to prove the law at school.

Boyle's own empirical results relating pressure directly to volume were only obtained in defending his earlier and more general "Doctrine touching on the Spring and Weight of Air." Indeed, his results relate only to air as such, which he studied in one type of apparatus of at least two sizes because the smaller one broke, and he spent much time explaining away his (small) discrepancies. But the relationship $P=k/V$ became established as a general "law" only a good deal later, because Boyle's initial work had then been followed by vast and laborious amounts of extremely repetitive and tiresome empirical data collection and analysis: the behaviour of this kind of gas and that kind of gas had been examined, under almost unbearably innumerable different conditions. To repeat: Large amounts of gas and small amounts of gas have been studied. And one kind of container and another kind of container. Pressure going up and pressure going down. Pressure going up fast and pressure going down slowly. And so on and so on. If the law is also known to hold to a close approximation at different times and for different places, this is only because of all the massive and direct empirical observation that something like it has in fact held here and there, in the morning and at night, this year and last year, and so on.

All the cases where the law does NOT hold involve still further work, further empirical observation and analysis. Thus it is very much a part of really establishing Boyle's Law to have shown empirically that $P=k/V$ does NOT hold when the temperature changes, or when there is a leak in the apparatus, or when there is a chemical reaction or physical condensation —and it has of course also been empirically established that these failures occur for this kind of gas and for that kind, for large amounts of gas and for small ones, and so on.

The apparent *simplicity* of many scientific laws is only a reflection of all the work which has been done empirically to rule out the complicating conditions where the simple result does NOT hold (changing temperature, leaks, etc.). The *power* of a law depends on the extent to which theoretical analysis has shown it to interrelate with other empirical laws and with general background knowledge. But the *validity* of a scientific law depends only on its range of empirical generalisation, i.e., the different conditions for which it is known to hold or not to hold, as shown by direct observation and analysis.

The same approach of course applies to laws in marketing. All that is necessary is to isolate simple regularities in marketing processes by observing and analysing the extent to which they do or do not occur under all the different conditions of observation which are at all relevant—different products, different brands, different countries and different times, and varying marketing conditions generally. Instead of the common doubts of the "Will it hold over extended time-periods?" or "Will so-and-so matter?" kind, we only need observe and analyse whether or not it does.

To establish generalised laws, we therefore have the basic law of scientific methodology:

> *The Basic Law of Methodology:* "If in doubt, find out."
> *Corollary:* "If you don't, you won't."

Some illustration of empirical marketing laws derived by this old-fashioned approach may be relevant. Three examples are given. Two are taken from papers published last month, the third is from some much more recent work.

The examples concern general laws from three fields: media, consumer attitudes, and purchasing behaviour. They illustrate that although the marketing laws which we can establish at this stage are of course much simpler than the complex laws which are now current in the natural sciences, there is no difference in kind. The complexity of the present-day laws in physics is due to the very much larger amount of work which has already gone into studying the subject-matter there: the physicist already knows so much more, but does not always have the mathematics to describe it very simply and concisely.

The first example of a simple empirical marketing law concerns some recent results on the viewing patterns of television audiences, as relating for instance to work for JICTAR, and C-E-I-R Inc., and ARB. I hasten to add that the example does not concern itself with the popular O.R. kinds of "media model" which are meant to optimise something. Instead, it is an example of establishing what actually happens, by way of "duplicated" viewing of any TV channel or station at any two specific times on any two different days of any week. For instance, given that 30 per cent of the population view on Monday night at 8 p.m., and that on Tuesday night at 9 p.m. the "rating" is 20 per cent, what is the duplicated audience at these two times, i.e., how many per cent of the population view the station both on Monday night at 8 and on Tuesday at 9?

The traditional view of "everything in marketing is complex and variable" is of course readily countered by simply looking at some actual duplication data. Examination of any table of the duplicated audiences for two days of the week makes the existence of a regular pattern almost immediately obvious. Thus for some recent data collected by the American Research Bureau, this pattern could be summarised as follows:

(i) The higher the rating at one time, the higher the duplicated audience with any other point in time.
(ii) The tendency for people who view at one time also to view at another time is positive, i.e., there is positive correlation.

(iii) This correlation can virtually all be accounted for by a single constant. Thus the duplicated audience d_{ts} at times t and s with ratings r_t and r_s is given by the simple law

$$d_{ts} = k\, r_t\, r_s,$$

where k is a constant.

(iv) The law $d_{ts} = k\ r_t\ r_s$ holds for the data in question with deviations averaging at a rating point or so. (The larger deviations which occur within these small average limits are not only rare but tend themselves to be highly regular, ie, susceptible to further lawlike description.)

The data analysed here refers to the audience to station WRBC on Mondays and Tuesdays in November last year in the Birmingham, Alabama, market. It may seem absurd to describe some apparent regularities in Alabama last November as a "law." Will such a result also hold for other pairs of days, and at other points in time, for other stations or in other places, and under other conditions generally? "If in doubt, find out." All that has to be done is to observe and analyse some comparable data for other points in space and time and for other conditions generally.

Other analyses have therefore also been carried out. They cover so far some sets-switched-on and housewife-viewing data measured by Television Audience Measurement in the London Region in January of 1966, and the earlier 1959 Granada Viewership Surveys of the adult population of Great Britain. Space and time (including seasons) are therefore beginning to be covered, as are also different "kinds of gas" (i.e., the viewing behaviour of individual people and of TV-sets), and different measurement techniques (ARB's weekly household diaries, Tam's continuous minute-by-minute meter and $\frac{1}{4}$-hour diary panels, and Granada's individual 7-day aided recall interviews). Even the few hundred cases analysed so far, therefore, begin to cover quite a wide range of empirical conditions, as set out in Table 1. And the same simple law—that $d_{ts} = k\ r_t\ r_s$—continues to emerge.

The second illustration of a simple law concerns an attitudinal variable, namely people's expressed Intentions-To-Buy any stated brand. In work for J. Walter Thompson, no evidence has been found that this variable measures what it says it measures, e.g., that it correlates or predicts changes in people's buying behaviour (Bird, *et al.*, 1966).

There is of course nothing unusual or wrong about that (as long as one knows). After all, in physics and in everyday life one does not look at the length of a column of mercury in a glass tube just to see how long a column of mercury in a glass tube is, but as a measure of something quite different—temperature or pressure, or whatever it is that empirical validation has told us the length of this particular type of mercury column is correlated with.

In thus empirically investigating the percentage I of people who express an Intenton-To-Buy the brand in question, it was found that

TABLE 1

Empirical Conditions Under Which $d_{ts} = k\, r_t\, r_s \pm 1$ Is Known to Hold*

Any two programs
Any two ratings levels from 0 to about 50
Any two times of day from 2 p.m. to 11:30 p.m.

Adults
Housewives
Sets-on

Continuous meter panels
Continuous diary panels
1-week diary surveys
1-week recall surveys

1959, 1965, 1966

Summer/Winter

London, ITV
Great Britain, ITV
Alabama, WRBC

Two-channel
Poly-channel**

*d_{ts} is the duplicated audience at two times t and s on two different days of the week with ratings r_t and r_s.
**The phrase "poly-channel" has been devised by Mr. N. L. Webb to distinguish multi-channel viewing situations with three or more operating channels from the two-channel situation which has been traditional in Great Britain until recently.

this variable tends to be systematically and closely related to the current Usership level of the brand. Thus I is directly proportional to the square root of the percentage U of informants who currently use the brand, i.e.,

$$I = k\sqrt{U},$$

within a mean deviation of about 3 percentage points for the discrepancies $|I - k\sqrt{U}|$ on the 0 per cent to 100 per cent scale of Intentions-To-Buy. This simple relationship between I and U, which has already been briefly quoted by Ramond (1965), is known to hold under the wide range of empirical conditions in Table 2. Thus, $I = k\sqrt{U}$ holds for large brands and small brands in each product-field and for brands with stationary and with fluctuating usage levels. It holds, with different values of the single parameter k, for some 30 different product-fields investigated by JWT so far and for various different measuring techniques. It holds at different points in time stretching back over five years or more and in Great Britain and in the U.S.

TABLE 2

Empirical Conditions Under Which $I = k\sqrt{U} \pm 3$ Is Known to Hold*

Intentions-To-Buy levels ranging from 0% to almost 100%
The 4 to 10 leading brands in each product-field
Brands with stationary usage level Brands with increasing usage level Brands with decreasing usage level
Great Britain U.S.A.
Demographic Subgroups (young, old, etc.)
From 1960 to 1966 Summer/Winter
Usage measures varying from "Ever Use" to "Used in last 7 days"
Several Intentions-To-Buy measures
Different product-fields including Beer, Biscuits, Breakfast Cereals, Chocolate Bars, Cigarettes, Corned Beef, Cough Syrups, Frozen Foods, Indigestion Remedies, Margarine, Meat Extracts, Milk Drinks, Shampoos, Tinned Soups, Toilet Paper, Toilet Soap, Voluntary Grocery Chains, Washing Powders, Washing-up Liquids

*I is the % of informant expressing an Intention-To-Buy a brand which is Used by U%.

The law differs from the first example $d_{ts} = k\ r_t\ r_s$—the duplication law—by already fitting in with other pieces of knowledge. For example, it quantifies the common notion that people cannot effectively say what they want (except more of the same), and it seems to clash with various speculative consumer theories of advertising formulated as sequences of the awareness→intention→purchase kind.

At a more down-to-earth level, it is also known (a) that current users of a brand virtually all say that they intend to buy it again, and (b) that for current non-users such an intention varies with the recency or the frequency of their *past* usage (if any) of the brand. This additional empirical knowledge (Bird, *et al.*, 1966) explains the shape of the $I = k\sqrt{U}$ type of relationship.

It also explains two systematic deviations from the $I = k\sqrt{U}$ norm which would otherwise appear quite paradoxical. These deviations occur within the average limits of fit of ± 3 per cent and apply to successfully launched new brands and to slowly dying old brands respectively, as follows:

(i) *Fewer* people than the norm say they intend to buy successful new brands (but more and more people do in fact buy them subsequently).

stationary brand of—to be specific—margarine like "Parkay," "Allsweet," "Good Luck," and "Nutley," or a stationary brand of detergent like "American Family Flakes," "Tide," and "Rinso" (pack-sizes I and II) in one time-period but not the next, also bought on average of roughly 1.4 units. Thus,

Quarterly: buying in one quarter, but not the next, the Average amount bought = 1.4 units;

Monthly: buying in one month, but not the next, the Average amount bought = 1.5 units.

These data are subject to considerable sampling error since the number of such buyers in Brown's samples was only about 5 to 10 per brand, but the fit seems good enough!

The above results illustrate that it is easy to find stable and simple laws in marketing. However, it would be disingenuous and indeed misleading to pretend that many such laws have yet been established. Very little integrated and generalised quantitative knowledge about marketing processes exists so far. For this situation, four quite unnecessary laws appear to be causally responsible.

The Law of Personal Pessimism: "In *my* case, nothing ever remains the same."

The Law of Empirical Inaction: "If still in doubt, just assume something."

The Law of Perpetually Promising Pseudo-Probabilistic Paraphernalia: "It is a well-known statistical procedure and may this time give a clearcut and lasting result."

The Law of the Ignorant Problem-Solver: "I know nothing of your subject-matter, but have techniques and will sub-optimise."

For further reading on these four laws, the initial reference and textbooks on "modern" scientific method and experimental design, on multivariate analysis, Bayesian theory and statistical analysis and inference generally, and on O.R. techniques may be helpful.

The discussion following the original delivery of this paper has shown that there are three further laws of inhibition which had been prematurely pensioned-off. They are, of course:

The Law of the Man of Action: "I am too busy pretending to solve today's problems to tackle tomorrow's before it is again too late."

The Law of the Practical-Minded Manager: "I cannot invest in research unless I know how to apply the results before you know what they are."

The Law of Keeping Secrets from Oneself: "We must keep the results from our competitors even if it means not getting them ourselves."

These seven laws seem to account for most of the near-constant tendency to do virtually no long-term basic research into marketing phenomena. This particular finding holds in Britain, in the U.S.A., and elsewhere, and so far also across time.

REFERENCES

Bird, M. & Ehrenberg, A. S. C. (1966). "Intentions-to-Buy and Claimed Brand Usage." *Op. Res. Quarterly*, **17**, March, 353-372, and **18**, 65-66.
Buzzell, R. D. (1963). "Is Marketing a Science?" *Harvard Business Review*, **41**, 1, 32-36.
Brown, G. H. (1952). "Brand Loyalty—Fact or Fiction?" *Advertising Age*, **23** (June 9 and October 6).
Chatfield, C., Ehrenberg, A. S. C. & Goodhardt, G. J. (1966). "Progress on a Simplified Model of Stationary Purchasing Behaviour." Read before the Royal Statistical Society, March 16th. *J. Roy. Statist. Soc. A.*, **129**, 317-367.
Langhoff, P. (Ed.) (1965). *Models, Measurement and Marketing*. New York: Prentice-Hall.
Ramond, C. K. (1965). "Editorial." *J. Adv. Research*, **5**, 4 (December), 68.

Appendix

Ethical Issues and Problems: A Series of Position Papers

Adopted July 1968 by THE MARKET RESEARCH COUNCIL*

THE RESPONDENT'S RIGHT TO PRIVACY

The goodwill and cooperation of the public are necessary to successful public opinion and market research. Actions by researchers which tend to dilute or dissipate these resources do a disservice both to the research profession and to the public.

By its very nature, research must in some measure invade the privacy of respondents. The ringing of a respondent's doorbell or his telephone is an intrusion. If he agrees to participate in a study, his private world of attitudes, knowledge, and behavior is further invaded.

Researchers should recognize that the public has no obligation to cooperate in a study. Overly long interviews and subject matter which causes discomfort or apprehension serve to reduce respondent cooperation. When such interviews cannot be avoided, efforts should be made to explain the reasons to the respondent and to mitigate his anxieties to the extent possible.

One of the greatest invasions of the privacy of respondents is through the use of research techniques such as hidden microphones and cameras. When such a research technique has been used, a respondent should be told and, if the respondent requests it, any portion of the interview that serves to identify the respondent should be deleted.

Even after the respondent has been interviewed, his privacy is endangered while his interview is being coded, processed, and analyzed. Research agencies have the same responsibility as other professional groups to take all

---

*These papers, developed by the Council's Ethics Committee, represent a first step with the expectation that additional papers may be added as future developments warrant.

reasonable steps to insure that employees with access to these data observe the canons of good taste and discretion in handling this information.

Since public opinion and market researchers must infringe on the privacy of the public at several stages of the research process, it is unlikely that any set of rules or code of ethics can prevent abuses by unscrupulous or careless researchers, even though such abuses are inexcuseable. The best hope of maintaining an attitude of goodwill and cooperation among the public will depend on researchers':

1. Being constantly mindful of the problem;
2. Keeping in mind the recommendations above;
3. Doing everything in their power to inform the public of the benefits of market and opinion research.

MAINTAINING RESPONDENT ANONYMITY

Good and accurate research requires obtaining honest and frank expressions of opinions and beliefs. Respondents are more likely (a) to participate in a survey and (b) to speak honestly and frankly if they believe that they will remain anonymous and will not be called to account for their expressed opinions or stated behavior. For this reason, every researcher should do everything in his power to protect the anonymity of the people he interviews unless he obtains their permission to reveal their names.

This does not preclude follow-up contacts for further research or for verification purposes. However, if there seems to be a reasonable possibility that there will be contacts for any other purposes, it is incumbent on the researcher to warn the respondent of this possibility.

The researcher should be willing to make reasonable efforts to provide evidence on the authenticity of the interviews he has made, providing this does not subject the respondents to harassment.

DISCLOSURE OR RELEASE OF SURVEY RESULTS

Implicit in the nature of surveys is the fact that they purport to reflect the opinions or behavior of the population under study. It is the obligation of the researcher to present survey results in such a manner that they do not give a distorted or biased picture of his findings. The client also has this same obligation in reporting survey findings. When others report his findings, the researcher has an additional responsibility to make all reasonable effort to see that they, likewise, present the results impartially.

It is not incumbent on the researcher to insist on an "all-or-nothing" policy in the release of his findings. Only part of the results may be released provided this part does not give a distorted picture of the subject matter it covers.

If the client misuses, misstates, or distorts a survey finding, the researcher should release such other findings and information about how the data were obtained as will put it in proper perspective. Client-researcher agreement prior to release would minimize misunderstandings in this respect.

Any release of findings should include appropriate information about objectives, sample, research techniques, the name of the research organization, etc., that will be helpful in evaluating the results.

BUYER-SELLER RELATIONSHIPS

A successful marketing research study is a joint operation involving a research company and its client. It requires mutual respect and confidence between the two parties and imposes certain obligations on each of them.

The buyer of research services has the right to make sure that the work he has contracted for meets all the specifications. He has the right to examine all operations of the research company to see that they are being carried out in the manner agreed upon. However, in doing so he should respect the research company's obligations to the public in matters of anonymity and invasion of respondents' privacy.

The buyer should recognize that the research company is a professional organization engaged in collecting marketing and/or opinion data. The buyer should not, therefore, ask or expect the research company to violate any of the suggested rules of procedure covered elsewhere in this statement. The buyer should not publicly identify the research agency in any release of findings, employing the endorsement of the research agency, without prior agreement from the agency.

It is understood that in seeking a research agency the buyer may request proposals from more than one research company. However, generating ideas and planning research designs to solve specific problems are an important part of the services a research agency offers. The buyer, therefore, should not (1) lift ideas from one proposal and give them to another research agency or (2) ask for a proposal from a company which he knows has little or no chance of obtaining his business, unless he so informs them in advance. Soliciting bids for the purpose of obtaining free ideas which will be turned over to another bidder, or for purely technical compliance with a company's policy of obtaining competitive bids, does a disservice to the research firms involved, reflects on the integrity of the client company, and generally lessens the professional level of the research profession.

Kickbacks, rebates, and other "inducements" similarly destroy the professional character of research and should not be solicited, offered, or agreed to.

The research agency has the obligation to express, as they become apparent, any reservations about the usefulness of the proposed research in solving the client's problem. The agency also has the obligation, of course, to do the study contracted for in the manner agreed on. No additional questions designed for another purpose should be included in interviews done for a client without the client's knowledge and consent.

Unless otherwise agreed on by the seller and the buyer, the study report and the compiled tabulated data on which it is based are the property of the buyer. No by-product information should be sold to another buyer unless express permission is obtained from the original buyer.

In the course of conducting research, the researcher may become privy to confidential information relating to the client company. The researcher should not reveal any of this material to any outsider at any time.

INFORMATION TO BE INCLUDED IN THE RESEARCH FIRM'S REPORT

Every research project differs from all others. So will every research report. All reports should nonetheless contain specific reference to the following items:

1. The objectives of the study (including statement of hypotheses);
2. The name of the organization for which the study is made and the name of the organization that conducted it;
3. Dates the survey was in the field and date of submission of final report;
4. A copy of the full interview questionnaire, including all cards and visual aids, used in the interview; alternatively, exact question wording, sequence of questions, etc.;
5. Description of the universe(s) studied;
6. Description of the number and types of people studied:
   a. Number of people (or other units),
   b. Means of their selection,
   c. If sample, method of sample selection,
   d. Adequacy of sample representativeness and size,
   e. Percentage of original sample contacted (number and type of call-backs),
   f. Range of tolerance,
   g. Number of cases for category breakouts,
   h. Weighting and estimating procedures used.

Where trend data are being reported and the methodology or question wording has been changed, these changes should be so noted.

On request—clients and other parties with legitimate interests may request and should expect to receive from the research firm the following:

a. Statistical and/or field methods of interview verification (and percentage of interviews verified);
b. Available data *re* validation of interview techniques;
c. Interviewing instructions;
d. Explanation of scoring or index number devices.

Marketing Research Code of Ethics

AMERICAN MARKETING ASSOCIATION

The American Marketing Association, in furtherance of its central objective of the advancement of science in marketing and in recognition of its obligation to the public, has established these principles of ethical practice of marketing research for the guidance of its members. In an increasingly complex society, marketing management is more and more dependent upon marketing information intelligently and systematically obtained. The consumer is the source of much of this information. Seeking the cooperation of the consumer in the development of information, marketing management must acknowledge its obligation to protect the public from misrepresentation and exploitation under the guise of research.

Similarly the research practitioner has an obligation to the discipline he practices and to those who provide support for his practice—an obligation to adhere to basic and commonly accepted standards of scientific investigation as they apply to the domain of marketing research.

It is the intent of this code to define ethical standards required of marketing research in satisfying these obligations.

Adherence to this code will assure the users of marketing research that the research was done in accordance with acceptable ethical practices. Those engaged in research will find in this code an affirmation of sound and honest basic principles which have developed over the years as the profession has grown. The field interviewers who are the point of contact between the profession and the consumer will also find guidance in fulfilling their vitally important role.

FOR RESEARCH USERS, PRACTITIONERS AND INTERVIEWERS

1. No individual or organization will undertake any activity which is directly or indirectly represented to be marketing research, but which has as its real purpose, the attempted sale of merchandise or services to some or all of the respondents interviewed in the course of the research.
2. If a respondent has been led to believe, directly or indirectly, that he is participating in a marketing research survey and that his anonymity will be protected, his name shall not be made known to anyone outside the research organization or research department, or used for other than research purposes.

FOR RESEARCH PRACTITIONERS

1. There will be no intentional or deliberate misrepresentation of research methods or results. An adequate description of methods employed will be made available upon request to the sponsor of the research. Evidence that field work has been completed according to specifications will, upon request, be made available to buyers of research.
2. The identity of the survey sponsor and/or the ultimate client for whom a survey is being done will be held in confidence at all times, unless this identity is to be revealed as part of the research design. Research information shall be held in confidence by the research organization or department and not used for personal gain or made available to any outside party unless the client specifically authorizes such release.
3. A research organization shall not undertake marketing studies for competitive clients when such studies would jeopardize the confidential nature of client–agency relationships.

FOR USERS OF MARKETING RESEARCH

1. A user of research shall not knowingly disseminate conclusions from a given research project or service that are inconsistent with or not warranted by the data.
2. To the extent that there is involved in a research project a unique design involving techniques, approaches or concepts not commonly available to research practitioners, the prospective user of research shall not solicit such a design from one practitioner and deliver it to another for execution without the approval of the design originator.

FOR FIELD INTERVIEWERS

1. Research assignments and materials received, as well as information obtained from respondents, shall be held in confidence by the interviewer and revealed to no one except the research organization conducting the marketing study.
2. No information gained through a marketing research activity shall be used, directly or indirectly, for the personal gain or advantage of the interviewer.
3. Interviews shall be conducted in strict accordance with specifications and instructions received.
4. An interviewer shall not carry out two or more interviewing assignments simultaneously unless authorized by all contractors or employers concerned.

* * *

Members of the American Marketing Association will be expected to conduct themselves in accordance with the provisions of this Code in all of their marketing research activities.

Code of Professional Ethics and Practices

AMERICAN ASSOCIATION FOR PUBLIC OPINION RESEARCH

We, the members of the American Association for Public Opinion Research, subscribe to the principles expressed in the following code. Our goal is to support sound practice in the profession of public opinion research. (By public opinion research we mean studies in which the principal source of information about individual beliefs, preferences, and behavior is a report given by the individual himself.)

We pledge ourselves to maintain high standards of scientific competence and integrity in our work, and in our relations both with our clients and with the general public. We further pledge ourselves to reject all tasks or assignments which would be inconsistent with the principles of this code.

THE CODE

I. Principles of Professional Practice in the Conduct of Our Work

A. We shall exercise due care in gathering and processing data, taking all reasonable steps to assure the accuracy of results.

B. We shall exercise due care in the development of research designs and in the analysis of data.

1. We shall employ only research tools and methods of analysis which, in our professional judgment, are well suited to the research problem at hand.
2. We shall not select research tools and methods of analysis because of their special capacity to yield a desired conclusion.
3. We shall not knowingly make interpretations of research results, nor shall we tacitly permit interpretations, which are inconsistent with the data available.
4. We shall not knowingly imply that interpretations should be accorded greater confidence than the data actually warrant.

C. We shall describe our findings and methods accurately and in appropriate detail in all research reports.

II. Principles of Professional Responsibility in Our Dealings with People

A. The Public:

1. We shall protect the anonymity of every respondent. We shall hold

as privileged and confidential all information which tends to identify the respondent.

2. We shall cooperate with legally authorized representatives of the public by describing the methods used in our studies.
3. We shall withhold the use of our name in connection with the planned publication of research findings unless we have first examined and approved the material.

B. Clients or Sponsors:

1. We shall hold confidential all information obtained about the client's general business affairs and about the findings of research conducted for the client, except when the dissemination of such information is expressly authorized.
2. We shall be mindful of the limitations of our techniques and facilities and shall accept only those research assignments which can be accomplished within these limitations.

C. The Profession:

1. We shall not cite our membership in the Association as evidence of professional competence, since the Association does not so certify any persons or organizations.
2. We recognize our responsibility to contribute to the science of public opinion research and to disseminate as freely as possible the ideas and findings which emerge from our research.

Code of Professional Ethics and Practices

WORLD ASSOCIATION FOR PUBLIC OPINION RESEARCH

I. Introduction

1. The World Association for Public Opinion Research (WAPOR), in fulfillment of its main objective to advance the use of science in the fields of public opinion and marketing research and in recognition of its obligations to the public, hereby prescribes principles of ethical practice for the guidance of its members, and a framework of professional standards which should be acceptable to users of research and to the public at large.

2. In an increasingly complex world, social and economic planning is more and more dependent upon marketing information and public opinion reliably studied. The general public is the source of much of this information. Consequently, members of WAPOR acknowledge their obligation to protect the public from misrepresentation and exploitation in the name of research. At the same time, WAPOR affirms the interdependence of free expression of individual opinion and the researcher's freedom to interview.

3. Members of WAPOR recognize their obligations both to the profession they practice and to those who provide support for this practice to adhere to the basic standards of scientific investigation.

4. This code defines professional ethics and practices in the field of opinion and marketing research. Adherence to this code is deemed necessary to maintain confidence that researchers in this field are bound by a set of sound and basic principles based on experience gained over many years of development.

II. Rules of Practice Between Research and Clients

A. *Responsibilities of Researchers*

5. The objective study of facts and data, conducted as accurately as permitted by the available resources and techniques, is the guiding principle of all research.

6. In executing his work, the researcher shall make every reasonable effort to adhere exactly to the specifications proposed to and accepted by the client. Should the researcher find it necessary to deviate from these specifications, he shall obtain the client's prior approval.

7. The researcher shall in every report distinguish his actual data from observations or judgments which may be based on other evidence.

8. The researcher shall not select tools of data collection and analysis because of the likelihood that they will support a desired conclusion, if that conclusion is not scientifically warranted.

9. Whenever data from a single survey are provided for more than one client or when data are provided to several clients, the researcher shall inform each client of the fact.

10. In the course of a field survey, the researcher shall not reveal the name of his client to respondents or to anyone else, unless authorized by the client.

11. All information and material supplied by the client for the research must remain confidential.

12. Without prior consent of the client, no findings from the commissioned research shall be disclosed by the researcher. However, unless there is agreement to the contrary, the research techniques and methods, such as sampling designs, names of interviewers, field instructions, etc., used for the study remain the researcher's property, if he has developed them.

13. Except by mutual consent, data shall not be sold or transferred by either the client or the researcher to parties not involved in the original contract work.

14. Unless it is customary or specifically agreed to the contrary, all punched cards, research documents (such as interviews and tests of sampled households) or any other material used in the field work shall be the property of the researcher. The practitioner is, however, required to provide for storage of this material for whatever period is customary in a particular country. This obligation shall be considered fulfilled by storage in a recognized data archive, if necessary, with restricted access.

15. Upon completion of a research study and after the researcher has submitted his final report, the client may request, according to previously mutually agreed specifications, a duplicate set of all punched cards prepared from the questionnaire, provided that the client shall bear the reasonable cost of preparing such duplicates, and that respondents remain unidentified.

16. The practitioner shall be accurate in providing prospective clients with information about his experience, capacities and organization.

B. *Responsibilities of Clients*

17. Potential clients asking for research proposals and quotations recognize that, in the absence of a fee being paid, such proposals and quotations remain the property of the researcher. In particular, prospective clients must not use the proposals of one practitioner competitively in order to obtain a lowering of the price from other practitioners.

18. Reports provided by the practitioner are normally for the use of the client and his agents. The researcher and the client shall agree in writing regarding the means of any wider dissemination of the complete or partial results of a research study.

In particular, it should be agreed that:

(a) The client shall ensure that any publication of survey results will not be quoted out of context or distort any facts or findings of the survey.

(b) The researcher must be consulted in regard to the form of publication and is entitled to refuse to grant permission for his name to be quoted in connection with the survey where he considers clause (a) has been violated.

C. *Rules of Practice Regarding Reports and Survey Results*

19. Every complete report on a survey should contain an adequate explanation of the following relevant points:

(a) for whom the survey was conducted;
(b) the purpose of the study;
(c) the universe or population to which the results of the survey are projected;
(d) the method by which the sample was selected including both the type of sample (probability, quota, etc.) and the specific procedures by which it was selected;
(e) steps taken to insure the sample design would actually be carried out in the field;
(f) the degree of success in actually carrying out the design including the rate of non-response and a comparison of the size and characteristics of the actual and anticipated samples;
(g) a full description of the estimating procedure used for all results which are reported including the sample size on which it was based and weighting procedures used to adjust raw data;
(h) a full description of the method employed in the field work;
(i) the time at which the field work, if any, was done, and the time span covered in collecting data;
(j) the findings obtained;
(k) (where the nature of the research demands it) the characteristics of those employed as interviewers and coders and the methods of their training and supervision;
(l) a copy of the interview schedule or questionnaire and instructions.

20. Technical terms shall be employed in a survey report in accordance with their commonly understood scientific usage.

III. Rules of Practice Between Researcher and Respondents

D. *Responsibility to Informants*

21. No informant or respondent must be adversely affected as a result of his answers or of the interviewing process. The practitioner shall use no methods or techniques by which the informant is put in the position that he cannot exercise his right to withdraw or refuse his answers at any stage of the interview.

22. No response in a survey shall be linked in any way to an identifiable respondent. The anonymity of respondents shall be respected, except in

rare cases, with that respondent's specific permission. The interview method shall never be used as a disguise for a sales solicitation.

23. For Field Interviewers:

(a) Research assignments and materials received, as well as information obtained from respondents shall be held in confidence by the interviewer and revealed to no one except the research organization conducting the study.

(b) No information gained through a research activity shall be used, directly or indirectly, for the personal gain or advantage of the interviewer in his relations with the respondents.

(c) Field work shall be conducted in strict accordance with specifications. No field worker shall carry out more than one assignment in contact with the same respondents unless this is authorized by the research organization.

IV. Rules of Practice Between Researchers

24. The principle of fair competition as generally understood and accepted should be applied by all researchers, even in cases where they may be the sole operators in their country.

25. In their personal and business relationships, researchers will be governed by the tradition of common respect among colleagues in the same profession.

26. No outside pressure, political or commercial, can be used by a researcher or research organization to justify violation of this code.

27. Members shall not try to turn to account or put into evidence the fact of their membership of WAPOR as a token of professional competence. Membership implies no guarantee of qualification, but it does imply acceptance of this code.

WARNER MEMORIAL LIBRARY
EASTERN COLLEGE
ST. DAVIDS, PA. 19087